The Algorithm of Life

How Mathematical Thinking Solves Human Problems

Zachariah Sinkala

Zachariah Sinkala
First edition
ISBN: 979-8-9953055-3-8
Printed in the United States of America

Dedication

For everyone who was told they were "not a math person."
You were never bad at math. You were never given a reason to
care.

Introduction: The Geometry of Chaos

The Morning You Cannot Solve

It is 7:14 in the morning. You are already behind.

Your phone has delivered fourteen notifications since you woke up—two from a work application, three from a group chat that never seems to sleep, one from a news app whose headline has already triggered a low-grade alarm somewhere in your chest, and several more you haven't opened yet because something about the number itself feels threatening. You have not had coffee. You have not had a moment of silence. And somewhere, beneath the noise, is a list of things you need to do today, a longer list of things you have been meaning to do for weeks, and an even longer list of things you are worried about but cannot quite name.

By 7:14 in the morning, most modern adults have already experienced more informational inputs than a person living a century ago would encounter in a week. We are living in the most information-rich environment in human history—and yet, by almost any measure, we are not making better decisions. We are more anxious, less focused, more reactive, and more uncertain about the direction of our lives than generations that had access to a fraction of what we carry in our pockets.

This is not a crisis of information. It is a crisis of framework.

The problem is not that you have too much data. The problem is that you have never been given a reliable system for processing it. You have been handed a hundred variables and no equation. And without an equation, even the most intelligent person defaults to the only tool that feels immediately available: **emotion.**

Emotion is not the enemy. It is ancient, efficient, and occasionally correct. But it was designed for a world of immediate physical threats—predators, famines, tribal conflict—not for the abstract, probabilistic, long-horizon problems that define modern life. When you use a fear response to navigate a career decision, or use social approval to evaluate a financial choice, you are using a biological instrument for a purpose it was never designed to serve. The results are predictable: paralysis, inconsistency, regret, and the nagging sense that you are working hard while going nowhere.

This book is an argument that there is a better operating system. And it has been sitting in your high school textbooks, misrepresented, underutilized, and dismissed, for your entire life.

The Greatest Miseducation in History

Ask most adults about their relationship with mathematics and you will hear a story with a remarkably consistent shape. It begins with early curiosity—counting, shapes, the satisfying click of a correct answer—and then somewhere around middle school, something shifts. The problems become abstract. The stakes become social. A test goes badly. A teacher moves too fast. And a belief takes root, quietly but durably: *I am not a math person.*

This belief is one of the most consequential fictions of modern education.

It is a fiction not because everyone has equal natural aptitude for symbolic manipulation or number theory. Some people genuinely find the higher registers of pure mathematics more accessible than others, just as some people find music or language or spatial reasoning more intuitive. Individual variation is real. But the belief "I am not a math person" rarely refers to Fourier analysis or algebraic topology. It refers to something much more basic: the sense that the logical, structured, evidence-based way of thinking that mathematics trains is somehow not available to you. That it belongs to a category of person you are not.

This belief is almost always wrong. And its consequences extend far beyond any classroom.

When you cannot think probabilistically, you make financial decisions based on how an outcome *feels* rather than how likely it is. You buy high because the mood is euphoric and sell low because the mood is fearful—the precise opposite of what the math recommends. When you cannot think in terms of systems and constraints, you try to solve problems by adding effort without analyzing structure, working longer hours without examining whether the hours are pointed in the right direction. When you cannot think in terms of compounding, you undervalue consistency and overvalue intensity, abandoning the slow processes that would have transformed your life if you had simply refused to stop.

The cost of mathematical illiteracy is not that you cannot calculate. It is that you cannot *see*. And what you cannot see, you cannot change.

What Mathematical Thinking Actually Is

Before we go further, we need to clear up a persistent misunderstanding about what this book is asking of you.

Mathematical thinking is not arithmetic. It is not the memorization of formulas, the execution of algorithms, or the performance of calculation. These are the surfaces of mathematics—the visible outputs of an underlying practice that is far more interesting and far more universally applicable than any specific technique.

At its core, mathematical thinking is a **discipline of clarity.** It is the practice of demanding that a problem be precisely defined before you attempt to solve it. It is the habit of separating what you know from what you are assuming. It is the commitment to following evidence where it leads, even when the destination is inconvenient. It is the willingness to update your beliefs when new data arrives, rather than defending a position because you held it yesterday.

These are not mathematical skills in the technical sense. They are cognitive habits that mathematics, uniquely among the subjects we teach, trains with rigor and consistency. When a mathematician encounters an undefined term, they stop and demand a definition. When an equation produces an absurd result, they don't ignore it—they trace backward through every assumption until they find the error. When a proof requires a step they cannot justify, they do not skip it and hope no one notices. They sit with the discomfort of not knowing until the knowing arrives.

This discipline, applied to the problems of ordinary life, is transformative.

Consider how differently these two people approach the same situation. Both have been feeling financially stressed for months. Person A experiences this as a generalized weight—an ambient anxiety that colors their mood, affects their sleep, and occasionally erupts into arguments about money. They feel that they should "be better with money" but the feeling has no traction. It is a judgment without a variable. An intention without a structure.

Person B asks a different set of questions. Not "how do I feel about this?" but "what exactly is the problem?" They sit down and, for the first time, produce an exact accounting of income, fixed expenses, variable expenses, and the gap between them. They name the number. They identify the largest variable in the gap. They calculate how long, at current rates, before the situation becomes critical. They model what changes to which variables would close the gap within a defined timeline. By the end of an hour, they have not solved the problem—but they have *defined* it. And a defined problem is already, structurally, halfway solved.

The difference between these two people is not intelligence. It is not discipline or character or willpower. It is a framework.

Chaos Has a Shape

The title of this introduction is not decorative. Chaos—genuine, overwhelming, can't-see-the-floor chaos—does have a geometry. It has a structure, even when that structure is not immediately visible. And mathematics is, at its deepest level, the science of finding structure where none appears to exist.

In the physical sciences, this is literal. The motion of three gravitationally interacting bodies appears chaotic—unpredictable, sensitive to initial conditions, impossible to solve in closed form. Yet even this apparent chaos is governed by differential equations that describe it precisely. The chaos is not in the system. The chaos is in our incomplete description of the system. When we add enough precision to our model, patterns emerge.

The same principle applies to the chaos of human experience. Your financial stress appears chaotic—a tangle of income and expenses and habits and history and emotion. But underneath it is a structure of variables and relationships that responds to analysis. Your career feels directionless—a sequence of experiences without an organizing theme. But underneath it is a vector problem: a question of magnitude and direction that can be plotted, evaluated, and corrected. Your relationships feel mysterious and fragile—subject to forces you cannot predict. But underneath them are feedback loops and game-theoretic dynamics that respond to deliberate, structured intervention.

The geometry is there. The question is whether you have been given the tools to see it.

This book gives you those tools. Not in the abstract—not as theory to be admired and set aside—but in direct application to the domains where your life is actually lived.

The Cost of Living Without the Framework

Before we look at what mathematical thinking offers, it is worth sitting briefly with what its absence costs. Not in a spirit of accusation—the miseducation described above was not your fault. But clarity about the cost creates motivation for the change.

Time. Without optimization thinking, most people spend their most productive hours on activities that feel urgent but are structurally unimportant. They experience their day as a sequence of demands rather than a resource to be allocated. They work hard and finish exhausted, uncertain whether the effort was pointed in the right direction. The mathematics of constraints shows that this is not a character failing. It is a resource allocation problem—solvable, once the equation is written.

Money. Financial anxiety is the most prevalent form of chronic stress in the developed world. Yet personal finance, at its core, is one of the most tractable mathematical problems a person will ever face. The inputs are small in number: income, expenses, time, and rate of return. The relevant equations—compound growth, expected value, the Kelly Criterion—are not complicated. The barrier is almost never the math. It is the avoidance of defining the problem clearly, because a clearly defined problem demands a response, and a demanded response requires that you confront uncomfortable truths about your behavior.

Relationships. We tend to treat the quality of our relationships as a product of love, compatibility, and luck. But research in social psychology has demonstrated, repeatedly, that relationship outcomes are substantially predictable from measurable behavioral patterns. The ratio of positive to negative interactions. The tendency toward cooperative versus defensive communication. The speed of repair after conflict. These are variables. They respond to intervention. The person who understands this is not less romantic or less authentic—they are more capable of building and sustaining the connections that make life meaningful.

Career. The most common professional regret is not having worked in the wrong field. It is having worked in the right field with the wrong strategy—hard effort, misaligned direction. The vector insight is simple: magnitude without direction produces displacement of zero. No amount of hustle corrects for a fundamentally misoriented strategy. But a small correction in direction, applied early, can produce a dramatically different destination over a decade.

Mental health. Anxiety, in its most common non-clinical forms, is frequently a response to undefined threat. The mind, encountering a problem it cannot bound, treats it as boundless—and responds with proportional alarm. Naming a problem, assigning it a probability, identifying its variables, and constructing a response is not merely a practical exercise. It is a direct intervention in the biology of stress. Definition is calming. Structure is calming. The equation is not cold. It is, in many cases, the most compassionate thing you can offer a frightened mind.

What This Book Is—and What It Is Not

This book is not a textbook. You will not be tested on the formulas. There is no certification at the end, no credential to display. What you will find, in each chapter, is one mathematical principle applied carefully and completely to a domain of ordinary human experience—time, money, relationships, career, decision-making, information, investment, and education.

Each principle is introduced with enough mathematical grounding to make it precise, but no more. If you have not thought about mathematics since high school, you will not be lost. If you use mathematics professionally, you will recognize the concepts and, I hope, find their application to non-quantitative domains surprising and generative.

Each chapter ends with a **Logic Check**: three questions designed not to test your retention of the material but to force an honest translation of it into your own life. These questions are the most important part of each chapter. The framework is inert until it meets a real problem. The Logic Checks are the mechanism of that meeting.

This book is also not a self-help book in the conventional sense. It will not tell you to wake up at five in the morning, manifest your goals, or find your passion. It will not offer you a ten-step system guaranteed to transform your life in thirty days. It will offer you something more durable and, I believe, more honest: a set of **lenses** through which the problems you already face become clearer, smaller, and more tractable.

Lenses do not solve problems. You solve problems. The lenses only show you what is actually there.

How to Use This Book

Read it with a pen. Not to annotate the margins with appreciation, but to do the work. When a formula appears, pause and ask: what are my actual values for these variables? When an example is given, test whether it maps to your own situation. When a Logic Check arrives, answer it in writing—not in your head, where the answers are always more satisfying than they deserve to be.

Each chapter is self-contained. You can read them in order, which provides a cumulative arc from precision and constraint through probability and compounding to relationship, career, and capital. Or you can navigate directly to the domain that most urgently needs your attention. The index and table of contents are designed to support both approaches.

One last note. The equations in this book are real. They are not decorative. But they are also not the point. The equations are handles—concrete, unambiguous formulations of ideas that, in the abstract, are easy to agree with and easy to forget. When you can write the equation, you can examine the equation. You can ask which variable is limiting you, which assumption you have made incorrectly, which term you have been ignoring. The equation makes the idea *operational*. And operational ideas change lives in ways that abstract ideas never do.

You were told, at some point, that you were not a math person. This book is the rebuttal.

Let us begin.

A note on the mathematics: Every equation in this book can be understood without a calculator and without formal mathematical training. Where derivations would be helpful, they are provided in plain language in the body of the text. The goal is never computation. The goal is always **clarity of structure**— the habit of asking, before you act: what are the variables, what are the constraints, and what does the logic actually require?

Contents

Chapter 1

The Precision Mandate

"A problem well-defined is a problem half-solved."
—Charles Kettering

1.1 The Problem With "I Just Need to Do Better"

Somewhere in the last several months, you have probably said some version of the following sentence—either aloud to someone else, or silently to yourself in the ten quiet minutes before sleep:

"I really need to get my life together."

And then, with some combination of exhaustion and vague resolve, you went to sleep. And the next morning, the problem was exactly as large as it had been the night before. Maybe larger, because now there was also the guilt of having identified it and done nothing.

This is not a failure of motivation. It is not a character flaw. It is a **mathematical error.**

"I need to get my life together" is not a problem statement. It is not even close to a problem statement. It is a sentiment—a compressed expression of dissatisfaction that contains no defined target, no identified variables, no measurable current state, and no specified endpoint. It is the emotional equivalent of telling an engineer to "build something better." Without further specification, no work can begin. The most skilled engineer in the world cannot make progress on an undefined brief, because there is no way to know when progress has been made.

Your brain, presented with a problem of this form, does exactly what you would expect a sophisticated system to do with insufficient inputs: it loops. It revisits the problem repeatedly, checking whether new information has arrived, finding that it hasn't, and cycling back to a holding state of low-grade anxiety. This is not weakness. This is correct behavior for a system that has not yet received the data it needs to act. The anxiety is not pathological. It is a signal—specifically, a signal that the problem has not yet been defined.

The antidote is not willpower. It is not motivation, positive thinking, or a better morning routine. The antidote is **precision.**

In mathematics, an equation with undefined variables is not a hard equation. It is not even an equation. It is a notation that gestures in the direction of an equation without yet becoming one. Before any solving can occur, before any technique can be applied, every term must be defined. This is not a preliminary step that precedes the real work. This is, in many cases, most of the work.

The same principle governs every domain of human striving.

$$Success = (Target \times Time) + Constraints$$

Notice what this equation demands before it will yield a solution. A specific, numerical *Target*—not "more success" but a defined quantity of a defined thing. A bounded *Time* horizon—not "someday" but a deadline that makes the variable finite. An honest accounting of *Constraints*—the real limitations that wall the equation and, paradoxically, make it solvable. Remove any of these three components and you no longer have a goal. You have a wish.

The Precision Mandate is the foundation on which every other chapter in this book rests. You cannot optimize what you have not defined. You cannot calculate the probability of an outcome you have not specified. You cannot compound progress toward a destination you have not named. Before the machinery of mathematical thinking can engage, the problem must be made precise.

This chapter shows you how.

1.2 Why Vagueness Feels Safe (And Why It Isn't)

Before we examine the mechanics of precision, it is worth understanding why most people resist it. Because they do resist it—not consciously, but structurally. The vague goal persists not because people are lazy or undisciplined, but because vagueness provides a specific and valuable psychological service.

A vague goal cannot be failed.

"I want to be healthier" is immune to falsification. You cannot wake up on December 31st and determine with certainty that you have not achieved it, because the target was never specified. You can always tell yourself that you are *somewhat* healthier than you were, that the year had extenuating circumstances, that healthier is a journey rather than a destination. The vagueness functions as permanent protection against the verdict of failure. It is an insurance policy written in ambiguous language—one that, by its very terms, can never be invoked.

In psychology, this dynamic is related to what researchers call **self-handicapping**—the tendency to create conditions that provide a ready explanation for failure, thereby protecting self-esteem. A vague goal is a structural self-handicap. It protects you from the pain of a clearly defined loss, but it does so by making a clearly defined win impossible as well.

The cost, paid slowly and invisibly, is direction.

Without a defined target, there is no coherent way to choose between competing uses of your time. Every choice that might move you toward a vague goal is roughly equivalent to every other, because none of them can be evaluated against a specific criterion. Should you spend Saturday morning at the gym or taking an online course? Should you reach out to that contact or work on the project you've been putting off? In the absence of a defined target, these choices are made by mood, habit, and social pressure—the same forces that produced your current situation. The loop continues.

The transition from vague to precise is therefore not merely a planning exercise. It is an act of courage. It means accepting that you might, at some defined future point, be clearly, unambiguously wrong. It means making a commitment that can be kept or broken. It means entering a world where your effort has a direction, which means it also has a verdict.

This is uncomfortable. It is also the only path to actual change.

1.3 The Anatomy of a Well-Formed Problem

In formal mathematics and computer science, a **well-formed formula** is one that follows the syntactic rules of its system completely—every symbol defined, every operator applied correctly, every variable in scope. A formula that violates these rules is not a difficult formula. It is not a formula at all. It cannot be evaluated.

A well-formed life problem has a precise analogue. It contains four components, each of which is necessary and none of which is sufficient alone.

Component 1: The Current State (S_0)

Before you can navigate anywhere, you must know where you are. This sounds obvious, but it is almost universally skipped in the way people frame their problems. "I need to save more money" contains no information about how much is currently saved, what the income and expense structure looks like, or what the monthly delta between them is. Without S_0, the gap between present and goal cannot be calculated, and no realistic timeline can be constructed.

Establishing your current state requires measurement—and measurement is often the uncomfortable part. It means opening the bank statements. It means stepping on the scale. It means writing down the actual number of hours you spent last week in deep, productive work versus reactive busyness. The measurement feels like an accusation. It is not. It is a coordinate. You cannot navigate without it.

Component 2: The Target State (S^*)

This is the defined, measurable outcome you are trying to reach. The critical requirement is that S^* must be **falsifiable**—meaning there must exist a possible future moment at which you could determine, with certainty, whether you have achieved it or not.

"Be healthier" is not falsifiable. "Run a 5K in under 28 minutes by June 1st" is. "Improve my relationship with my partner" is not falsifiable. "Have one uninterrupted, screen-free dinner conversation per day for 30 consecutive days" is. "Get better at my job" is not falsifiable. "Reduce my average client response time from 48 hours to 12 hours by the end of the quarter" is.

The falsifiability requirement is not bureaucratic pedantry. It is the feature that makes the goal *actionable*. When S^* is falsifiable, you can at any moment calculate the gap between S_0 and S^* and ask the only productive question: what is the next specific action that reduces this gap?

Component 3: The Variables ($V_1, V_2, \ldots, V_n$)

Variables are the factors that genuinely influence the gap between S_0 and S^* and that are, at least in principle, within your capacity to change. Identifying them is a more exacting exercise than it first appears.

Most people's initial list of variables contains a mix of genuine levers and false ones. "My boss's attitude," "the economy," "my genetics," "whether my partner is supportive"—these may be real influences on your situation, but if you cannot directly change them, they are not variables in your equation. They are noise. Including them in your variable list feels legitimate—it acknowledges the real complexity of your situation—but it also quietly redistributes agency away from you and toward external forces. A variable list dominated by things you cannot control is an equation you cannot solve.

The discipline of the variable audit is to ruthlessly separate the factors you can move from the factors you cannot, and to focus exclusively on the former. This is not toxic positivity or denial of external reality. It is correct problem-solving. You acknowledge the existence of uncontrollable factors—they are part of your constraint set—but you do not waste cognitive resources on variables that have no levers.

Component 4: The Constraints ($C_1, C_2, \ldots, C_k$)

Constraints are the fixed parameters of your equation—the walls of the solvable space. Time is always a constraint: you have a finite number of hours. Capital is usually a constraint. Certain skills take time to develop and cannot be accelerated beyond biological limits. Geography, existing commitments, and physical capacity are constraints.

Here is the counterintuitive insight that mathematical thinking offers about constraints: **they are not obstacles to solving the problem. They are what makes the problem solvable.**

An equation with no constraints has infinite solutions. An optimization problem with no bounds is, technically, unbounded—meaning the "optimal" answer is always "more," which is no answer at all. The constraints are what create the structure within which a unique, actionable solution can be found. A person who says "I have no time, no money, and no connections" has actually provided the most important information in the analysis: the exact shape of the space within which a solution must exist. That space is smaller than an unbounded one. Smaller is easier to search.

When your constraints feel like the reason you cannot succeed, remember: they are the reason the problem has a solution at all.

1.4 The Cost of Vagueness: A Quantitative Look

Let us make concrete what the previous sections describe in principle. Consider two people, both 32 years old, both unhappy with their financial situation, both earning the same income. Both decide, at the start of a new year, to "save more money."

Person A carries this intention forward as stated. They feel, most months, that they should be putting money aside, and they sometimes do—a hundred dollars here, two hundred there, nothing in the months when an unexpected expense arrives. By December, they have saved an irregular, unplanned amount that does not correspond to any target and cannot be evaluated as success or failure. The intention has persisted for twelve months and produced an ambiguous outcome.

Person B applies the four-component framework on January 1st. Current state: $800 in savings, $3,400 monthly net income, $3,100 in monthly fixed and variable expenses, leaving a monthly surplus of $300 before discretionary spending. Target: $5,000 emergency fund by December 31st. Variables: discretionary spending (average $280/month), one recurring subscription that could be cancelled ($45/month), frequency of restaurant meals (average $180/month). Constraint: the $300 structural surplus is the ceiling without a change in income or fixed expenses. Required monthly savings to hit target: $\$5{,}000/12 \approx \$417$.

Person B has now identified a specific problem: the required savings rate ($417) exceeds the current structural surplus ($300) by $117. This means the target, as stated, requires either increasing income, decreasing fixed expenses, or reducing discretionary spending by at least $117 per month. The subscriptions and restaurant spending are the most accessible variables. The equation is now solvable.

Person A and Person B started with identical intentions and identical financial situations. By the end of January, Person B has a plan. Person A has a feeling. By December, their outcomes will not be identical.

1.5 The Language of Precision: Words That Destroy Equations

There is a category of language that functions as a solvent on precision—words and phrases that feel like planning but actively prevent the formation of a well-defined problem. Learning to recognize them, and immediately replace them with their precise equivalents, is one of the highest-leverage habits you can build.

"More" and "less." These are not targets. They are directions. "I want to exercise more" gives you no criterion for success, no way to measure progress, and no way to determine whether a given week's behavior counts. Replace with: "I will exercise four times per week for at least 35 minutes each session."

"Better" and "worse." Comparative terms with no specified baseline or endpoint. "I want to be a stronger communicator" could mean almost anything. Replace it with a specific behavioral definition: "I will respond to all client messages within four hours and follow up on open items weekly."

"Someday" and "eventually." These are not time horizons. They are deferrals. They convert a goal into a standing intention—something you can hold without acting on indefinitely. Replace with a date.

"Try" and "work on." These words specify process without specifying outcome, which means they can never be completed. You can "work on" a problem for a decade without resolving it. Replace with result-oriented language: not "I am working on improving my sleep" but "I will be asleep by 10:30pm on weekdays."

"Feel like" and "seem to." These are epistemic hedges that signal you have not yet measured the current state. They protect you from a confrontation with a number, which means they also prevent you from using the number. Replace by measuring. Not "I feel like I've been less productive lately" but "I tracked my deep work hours this week: 4.5 hours across five days."

Each time you replace a precision-dissolving phrase with a specific, measurable, time-bounded equivalent, you convert a vague intention into the beginning of an equation. And equations can be solved.

1.6 Precision Under Uncertainty: When You Don't Have All the Data

A common objection to the precision framework is that it seems to require complete information before action can begin—and real life rarely provides complete information.

Goals change. Circumstances shift. Committing to a specific target in January may feel premature because you don't yet know what March will bring.

This objection confuses **precision** with **certainty.** They are not the same thing.

Precision means your current best estimate is stated clearly and specifically, with an honest acknowledgment of your uncertainty. A meteorologist does not refuse to forecast because the future is uncertain. They give you a probability: 70% chance of rain. That forecast is precise—it specifies a quantity and an outcome—even though it is explicitly probabilistic. A navigator using dead reckoning before GPS did not refuse to plot a course because the ocean was unmapped. They calculated the best estimate from available data, committed to a heading, and updated as new information arrived.

The mathematical concept that governs this mode of operation is **iterative refinement.** You define the problem as precisely as current information allows, act on that definition, gather new data from the results, and revise the definition accordingly. The first definition does not need to be perfect. It needs to be precise enough to be testable—because a testable definition generates feedback, and feedback is the raw material of improvement.

This is why the Logic Check at the end of each chapter asks you to write things down. Writing forces precision. An idea that seems clear in your head will often reveal its vagueness the moment you attempt to commit it to a sentence. The resistance you feel when trying to write a specific numerical goal is not a sign that the goal is wrong. It is a sign that the process is working—that the vagueness that was previously invisible has become visible, and can now be corrected.

1.7 The Variable Audit: A Practical Protocol

The following protocol is designed to be applied to any significant life problem—financial, professional, relational, or personal—in a single focused session of thirty to sixty minutes. It is not a thought experiment. It requires paper (or a document) and actual numbers. Vague responses at any step indicate that more measurement is needed before the protocol can proceed.

Step 1: Name the domain.
Identify the single domain in which the problem lives. Resist the temptation to bundle multiple domains into one session. "My life is a mess" is not a domain. "My finances" is. "My career progression" is. "My physical fitness" is. If you cannot name the domain in three words, the problem has not yet been scoped.

Step 2: Measure the current state (S_0).
Write down the number that describes your present situation in the chosen domain. If you are addressing finances, this is your current net savings, your monthly income, and your monthly expenses—not approximately, but exactly. If you are addressing fitness, this is your current measurable performance on a chosen metric. If you cannot produce a number, you have identified your first action: measure.

Step 3: Define the target state (S^*).
Write down the specific, falsifiable outcome you want to achieve, with a date by which you intend to achieve it. Test it: could a neutral observer, on that date, definitively determine whether you achieved this or not? If yes, the target is well-formed. If not, make it more specific.

Step 4: Calculate the gap.

Compute $\Delta = S^* - S_0$. This is the magnitude of the problem. It may be larger or smaller than you expected. Either way, it is now a number—and numbers are workable. Feelings are not.

$$\Delta = S^* - S_0 \tag{1.1}$$

Step 5: List the variables.

Write down every factor that could reduce Δ and that you have direct capacity to influence. Be specific: not "work harder" but "increase billable hours from 28 to 35 per week." Not "eat better" but "reduce caloric intake by 300 calories per day by eliminating afternoon snacks." For each variable, estimate its magnitude of impact on Δ.

Step 6: List the constraints.

Write down the genuine, non-negotiable limits that bound your solution space. Be honest, but be rigorous. A constraint is something that genuinely cannot change within your time horizon—not something that would be inconvenient to change. "I can't work more hours" deserves scrutiny. "I have a legal obligation that occupies Tuesday evenings" does not.

Step 7: Identify the leverage variable.

Among all the variables you listed in Step 5, which single one, if maximally changed within your constraints, would produce the largest reduction in Δ? This is your primary lever. Everything else is secondary—not unimportant, but not your focus. Concentration of effort on the highest-leverage variable is the single most common differentiator between people who make rapid, visible progress and people who remain busy but unchanged.

The output of this protocol is not a plan. Plans are more detailed documents, built from a foundation of precise problem definition. The output is a **well-formed problem**: a statement that specifies where you are, where you want to be, by when, through which variables, within which constraints, with a single identified point of maximum leverage. This statement is the raw material from which every subsequent decision in the domain can be made rationally.

1.8 The Precision Mandate in Three Domains

To make this concrete, here is how the protocol transforms vague chronic frustrations into solvable problems across three domains that appear in later chapters.

Financial Precision

Vague version: "I need to stop living paycheck to paycheck."

Precise version: "My current monthly surplus after fixed expenses is \$220. My S^* is a \$4,000 emergency fund within 14 months, requiring \$286/month in savings. The gap between current surplus and required savings is \$66. My highest-leverage variable is dining spending (\$310/month average), which I will reduce to \$200/month, closing the gap and providing a \$44 buffer."

The vague version is a complaint. The precise version is an equation with a solution.

Career Precision

Vague version: "I feel stuck in my career and need to make a move."

Precise version: "I have been at my current level for 3 years with no promotion. The role above mine requires demonstrated project leadership and a specific technical certification I do not currently hold. My S^* is a promotion within 18 months. Variable 1: lead a cross-functional project (no current obstacle). Variable 2: obtain certification (12 weeks of study, 8 hours per week). Constraint: I have 10 available hours per week outside work obligations. This is sufficient for Variable 2 within the time horizon, assuming I begin within 30 days."

Relational Precision

Vague version: "My relationship doesn't feel as connected as it used to."

Precise version: "For the past six weeks, my partner and I have had fewer than two uninterrupted conversations per week and have not had a shared activity outside the home. My S^* is to re-establish a baseline of three meaningful interactions per week—one planned shared activity and two screen-free dinners—for a minimum of four consecutive weeks. Constraint: both schedules are full Tuesday through Thursday evenings. Available slots: Sunday afternoon, Monday evening, Saturday morning."

In each case, the act of precision does not solve the problem. What it does is reveal that the problem *is solvable*—that it has a specific shape, a specific gap, and specific levers. The problem has not gotten easier. It has become visible. And visible problems, unlike invisible ones, can be engaged.

1.9 The Compounding Value of Precision as a Habit

The benefits of applying the Variable Audit once are real but limited. A single session of precision thinking addresses one defined problem in one domain. The transformative value of the Precision Mandate accrues when it becomes a **default mode of cognition**—when the first response to any frustration, setback, or sense of stuckness is not an emotional reaction but a definitional one.

What exactly is the problem? What am I actually trying to achieve? What is measurable here? What can I change and what can't I?

This shift does not happen overnight. It is a habit, and habits require repetition before they become automatic. But the compounding effect is significant. A person who has practiced precision thinking for two years approaches a new problem differently at the level of reflex—before the emotional response has fully formed, the definitional questions are already running. The gap between feeling stuck and being able to act on the stuckness compresses from days to hours to minutes.

There is also a second-order benefit. Precision thinking, once practiced consistently, changes what you notice. You begin to hear the vague language in other people's problem statements—not with judgment, but with diagnostic clarity. "I feel like things aren't going well" immediately prompts the internal question: in what domain, by what measure, compared to what baseline? This makes you a more useful collaborator, a more effective manager, and a more patient listener, because you understand that the vagueness is not evasiveness—it is a problem of definition that you can help with.

The Precision Mandate is, in the end, an act of respect—for your own time, your own capacity, and the seriousness of your own goals. Vague goals are a form of self-dismissal. They say, implicitly, that the problem is too complex to be named, that the commitment is too frightening to be made, that the failure would be too painful to be risked. Precision says the opposite. It says: this matters enough to define. It matters enough to measure. It matters enough to risk being wrong about—because being wrong about a defined thing is the only path to eventually being right about it.

Write the equation. Even if the numbers are uncomfortable. Especially if the numbers are uncomfortable. The discomfort is the sensation of precision doing its work.

Chapter Logic Check

- ☐ What is my most persistent vague frustration right now—and can I restate it as a specific gap between a measurable S_0 and a falsifiable S^* with a date?

- ☐ Which words in my current goal language ("more," "better," "someday," "try") am I using as substitutes for a commitment I have not yet been willing to make?

- ☐ Among the variables I can genuinely influence in my highest-priority problem, which single one has the largest leverage on the gap—and what is the next concrete action on that variable?

Chapter 2

Algorithmic Living: Building Systems That Decide for You

"An algorithm must be seen to be believed."
—Donald Knuth

2.1 The Decision You Have Already Made a Thousand Times

Think about the last time you made coffee. Or buckled your seatbelt. Or responded to a message with "sounds good." You did not deliberate over any of these. You did not weigh competing options, consult your values, or feel the friction of uncertainty. You simply acted—smoothly, automatically, without expenditure of mental effort.

Now think about the last time you faced a genuinely hard decision. Not coffee versus tea, but whether to leave a job, end a relationship, confront a colleague, invest a significant sum, or commit to a direction for the next two years. How long did that decision take? How much energy did it consume? How many times did you return to it after you thought you had resolved it, find the same anxiety waiting, and begin the deliberation again from the beginning?

The difference between these two categories of experience is not the intrinsic difficulty of the problems. It is the presence or absence of a **system.**

Coffee is easy because you have already decided how to make it. The algorithm is installed. The inputs are recognized, the steps are sequenced, the output is consistent. Your conscious attention is not required and is therefore free for other work. The hard decision is hard not only because the stakes are higher, but because you have not yet built the decision architecture that would allow you to engage it systematically rather than emotionally, repeatedly, and exhaustingly.

This is the central insight of algorithmic living: the quality of your life is substantially determined not by your ability to make good decisions in the moment, but by the quality of the **systems** you have built to make recurring decisions on your behalf. A well-designed algorithm is not a shortcut. It is the most thorough form of preparation—thinking done in advance so that you do not have to think under pressure.

Chapter One taught you to define the problem. This chapter teaches you to build the machine that solves it consistently.

2.2   What an Algorithm Actually Is

The word "algorithm" has accumulated a layer of technological connotation that can make it feel inaccessible. In common usage, algorithms are things that happen inside computers and social media platforms—opaque, technical, not for ordinary people. This is a distortion. The concept predates computers by centuries and is, at its root, entirely mundane.

An **algorithm** is a finite, ordered sequence of unambiguous instructions that, when followed, produces a defined output from a given input. That is the complete definition. Notice what it does not require: a computer, specialized training, or any particular domain of application. Every recipe is an algorithm. Every medical triage protocol is an algorithm. Every checklist a pilot runs before takeoff is an algorithm. Every morning routine that reliably produces a person ready to work by a certain hour is an algorithm.

The three properties of the definition are each important.

Finite. The algorithm must terminate. A process that continues indefinitely—like rumination, or the endless reconsideration of a decision already made—is not an algorithm. It is a loop. One of the most valuable things a well-designed personal algorithm does is give rumination a stopping condition: a point at which the deliberation is complete and the output is committed.

Ordered. The steps have a sequence that matters. Reversing the order changes the output or breaks the process entirely. This property forces you to think carefully about dependencies—which decisions must precede which, and what information is required at each stage before the next can begin.

Unambiguous. Each instruction must be interpretable in exactly one way. "Exercise more" is not an algorithmic instruction. "Perform 25 minutes of Zone 2 cardio at 65–75% maximum heart rate on Monday, Wednesday, and Friday before 8:00 am" is. The unambiguity requirement is the link back to Chapter One: precision is not just a way of defining goals; it is the prerequisite for building systems that can pursue them without constant improvisation.

2.3　The Cognitive Cost of Living Without Algorithms

In 1999, social psychologist Roy Baumeister and colleagues published a series of experiments demonstrating that the capacity for self-control and deliberate decision-making is a depletable resource. They called the phenomenon **ego depletion**: the observation that making decisions, resisting temptation, and exercising willpower draws from a common pool of mental energy that diminishes with use. Later research complicated the exact mechanism, but the practical observation has held across many contexts: making decisions is cognitively expensive, and the quality of decisions tends to decline as the quantity increases.

This has a straightforward and often overlooked implication. Every decision you make manually—including decisions you have made hundreds of times before—draws from the same finite pool of cognitive resources you need for your most important work. The person who deliberates every morning about whether to exercise is spending decision-making capital on a question they have, presumably, already answered in principle. The person who deliberates each time about whether to check their phone during a focused work session is spending attention on a question that could have been resolved once, in advance, with a rule.

The mathematical framing is simple. Let D represent your daily decision-making capacity. Let R be the number of recurring decisions you make manually each day, each costing c_i units of capacity. Your remaining capacity for novel, high-stakes decisions is:

$$D_{\text{available}} = D_{\text{total}} - \sum_{i=1}^{R} c_i \qquad (2.1)$$

Every recurring decision you *algorithmize*—convert from a manual deliberation into an automatic execution—removes one c_i from the sum and returns that capacity to your available pool. This is not laziness. It is **cognitive resource management.**

Barack Obama famously wore only gray or blue suits during his presidency, eliminating clothing decisions entirely. Not because the decision was trivial—it is—but precisely because it was trivial, and trivial decisions have no business consuming the same mental resources as consequential ones. Steve Jobs, Mark Zuckerberg, and numerous other high-performers have implemented similar "uniform" policies in their daily routines, not as eccentricity but as deliberate reduction of $\sum c_i$. The logic is identical: automate the small so you can think clearly about the large.

> *Effective Judgment = Total Capacity − Cost of Recurring Decisions*

2.4 The Architecture of a Personal Algorithm

Building a personal algorithm is not a software engineering exercise. It does not require special tools, technical background, or even a particularly organized mind to begin. It requires only the willingness to apply the same precision you developed in Chapter One to a *process* rather than a *goal*.

A personal algorithm has four structural components.

Component 1: The Trigger Condition

Every algorithm begins with a signal that activates it. In computer science this is called a **conditional**: the logical structure IF [condition] THEN [execute process]. In daily life, trigger conditions are the specific, recognizable circumstances that call for a specific, pre-designed response.

The trigger must be *specific enough to be unambiguous* and *general enough to recur.* "When I feel stressed" is too vague to be a reliable trigger—the state is poorly defined, and its recognition is subject to emotional distortion. "When I have received a message that I feel angry about" is better: the event is concrete, its occurrence is recognizable, and the emotional state it produces is one in which a pre-committed algorithm is most valuable.

Identifying your triggers is partly a prospective exercise (what situations recur in my life that I tend to handle inconsistently?) and partly a retrospective one (looking back at the last month, which recurring situations most reliably produced outcomes I regretted?). The intersection of these two lists is your highest-priority algorithm target.

Component 2: The Decision Criteria

These are the explicit rules that determine the output of the algorithm given the input. They are where the thinking happens—but it happens *once, in advance,* when you are calm, well-rested, and not under the pressure of the situation itself.

Good decision criteria share the properties of a well-formed problem from Chapter One: they are specific, measurable, and falsifiable. Not "spend within my means" but "no discretionary purchase above $200 without a 48-hour waiting period and explicit budget reconciliation." Not "respond thoughtfully to difficult messages" but "do not respond to any message sent in anger within 60 minutes of receiving it; draft the response, wait, and review before sending."

The discipline of writing down your decision criteria in advance is simultaneously a planning exercise and a self-knowledge exercise. The process of trying to articulate a rule often reveals that you do not yet understand your own values clearly enough to formalize them. This is useful information. It means the algorithm-building process has identified a domain where more thinking is needed before systematic action can proceed.

Component 3: The Execution Sequence

Given that the trigger has been recognized and the decision criteria have returned an output, the execution sequence is the ordered set of specific actions that constitute the response. This is the part of the algorithm that most closely resembles a checklist.

Checklists have a complicated cultural reputation. In informal contexts they are associated with bureaucratic over-engineering—excessive structure imposed on situations that should be handled with judgment and experience. But surgeon and author Atul Gawande's landmark work on checklist use in surgical and aviation contexts documented something striking: in high-skill, high-experience professions where practitioners had performed a given procedure hundreds or thousands of times, the introduction of simple, well-designed checklists produced dramatic reductions in error rates. Not because the practitioners lacked competence, but because memory under pressure is unreliable and sequential task completion is cognitively demanding even for experts.

The personal execution sequence is your checklist for recurring situations. It does not replace judgment; it *preserves* judgment for the steps that genuinely require it, by automating the steps that do not.

Component 4: The Stopping Condition and Review Gate

Every algorithm must terminate, and every personal algorithm should include a scheduled review. The stopping condition is what concludes a single execution of the process. The review gate is a recurring calendar appointment—weekly, monthly, or quarterly, depending on the algorithm's domain—at which you evaluate the algorithm's performance: Is it producing the intended outputs? Have the circumstances that generated the trigger conditions changed? Does the execution sequence need modification?

This last component is what distinguishes a *living system* from a rigid rule. Rules are static; they apply until broken or abandoned. Algorithms are dynamic; they evolve through deliberate iteration. A personal algorithm that has not been reviewed in twelve months is, in all likelihood, no longer optimally calibrated to your current life. The review gate is the mechanism of adaptation.

2.5 Decision Trees: The If-Then Architecture of Daily Life

The most common structural form of a personal algorithm is the **decision tree**: a branching series of if-then conditions that maps a complex decision space into a navigable sequence of binary choices. Decision trees are used in medicine (diagnostic protocols), law (case resolution frameworks), finance (investment screening criteria), and machine learning—but their most immediate application requires no technology at all.

Consider the recurring decision of how to respond when someone makes a request of your time. Without an algorithm, this decision is made in real time, under social pressure, with incomplete information, and subject to all the cognitive distortions—people-pleasing, loss aversion, optimism bias—that govern decisions made emotionally. The result is frequently an inconsistency: sometimes you agree to things you should decline; sometimes you decline things you should accept; and in both cases, the decision is made on the basis of how you feel in the moment rather than on the basis of your actual priorities.

A time-commitment decision tree might look like this:

Level 1: Does this request align with at least one of my three current primary objectives?

- **No** → Decline. No further deliberation required.

- **Yes** → Proceed to Level 2.

Level 2: Do I have available capacity in the relevant time horizon without displacing a higher-priority commitment?

- **No** → Decline or defer with a specific future date.

- **Yes** → Proceed to Level 3.

Level 3: Am I the appropriate person for this task, or does someone else exist who could execute it with equal or greater effectiveness?

- **No, someone else is better positioned** → Refer and decline.

- **Yes, I am the right person** → Accept and schedule.

This tree does not make the decision for you in the sense of bypassing your judgment. It *structures* your judgment—forcing the relevant questions into the right sequence, ensuring that alignment with priorities is evaluated before availability, and that availability is evaluated before fit. The output is consistent with your stated values rather than with your mood at the moment of the request.

The same architecture applies across domains. A financial decision tree screens purchases against budget categories, time horizons, and opportunity cost before approval. A communication decision tree routes incoming messages to immediate response, scheduled response, or archive based on urgency and importance criteria. A health decision tree governs responses to the nightly question of whether to exercise, incorporating energy level, sleep data, and scheduling constraints into a reproducible answer rather than a nightly negotiation with motivation.

$$Output\ Quality = Decision\ Criteria \times Consistency\ of\ Application$$

2.6 The Habit Stack: Algorithms in Series

Individual algorithms govern individual recurring decisions. But the most powerful application of algorithmic thinking is the **habit stack**—a deliberately designed sequence of algorithms chained together so that the output of one becomes the trigger condition of the next.

The concept was popularized by behavioral psychologist BJ Fogg under the name "habit stacking," and its mechanism is straightforward: existing behaviors, reliably performed, are the most stable possible trigger conditions for new ones. The brain has already established the neural pathway that executes the existing behavior; attaching a new behavior to that pathway leverages an existing signal rather than requiring the construction of a new one.

In mathematical terms, a habit stack is a **composition of functions**. If behavior A reliably produces state σ_A, and the algorithm for behavior B is triggered by state σ_A, then the execution of A automatically initializes B:

$$f_B\big(f_A(x)\big) = f_{A \to B}(x) \tag{2.2}$$

The power of the composition is that the transition between A and B requires no new decision. The activation energy for B is supplied by the successful completion of A. This is why morning routines are so effective when designed correctly: each completed step creates the context for the next, reducing the total willpower expenditure to the cost of initiating the first step.

In practice, building a habit stack requires three design decisions: selecting the *anchor*—the existing, reliable behavior that opens the chain; specifying the *sequence*—the ordered behaviors that follow, each triggered by the completion of the previous; and establishing the *closing ritual*—a defined behavior that signals the end of the stack and releases attention to less structured activity.

A well-designed morning stack might be anchored by the act of making coffee (existing, automatic, reliable), followed by fifteen minutes of written planning triggered by the completion of coffee preparation, followed by the first work task triggered by the completion of planning. Each step is specific, sequenced, and requires only that the previous step complete—not that motivation be regenerated from scratch each morning.

2.7 When Algorithms Fail: Debugging Your Systems

Every algorithm, no matter how carefully designed, will eventually fail to produce its intended output. The trigger condition will occur but the execution sequence will not complete. The decision criteria will be applied but will return an inconsistent answer. The stopping condition will be reached but the loop will not terminate. These failures are not evidence that the algorithm was a bad idea. They are **diagnostic data.**

In software engineering, debugging is the process of tracing an unexpected output backward through the system to identify the point at which the logic diverged from intention. Personal algorithm debugging follows the same logic:

Type 1 – Trigger Failure: The algorithm was not activated even though the trigger condition was met. This usually indicates that the trigger was not specific enough—it was defined as a state or feeling rather than a concrete, observable event.

Fix: redefine the trigger as a specific, external, unambiguous event.

Type 2 – Criteria Failure: The algorithm activated but the decision criteria produced an output inconsistent with your values. This usually indicates that the criteria were written when your circumstances or priorities were different, and the algorithm has not been updated. Fix: schedule the overdue review gate and revise the criteria.

Type 3 – Execution Failure: The trigger activated, the criteria returned the correct output, but the execution sequence was not completed. This usually indicates one of two things: the sequence contains a step that is too effortful for the available energy state, or an unaccounted-for external condition blocked a step in the chain. Fix: audit the sequence for steps whose effort cost exceeds the typical available activation energy at trigger time; simplify or relocate them.

Type 4 – Stopping Failure: The algorithm activated and executed but did not terminate—the loop continued past its intended endpoint. This usually presents as rumination (a decision-making algorithm that continues reviewing the decision after it has been made) or perfectionism (an execution algorithm that continues refining the output after the quality threshold has been met). Fix: add an explicit, external stopping condition—a timer, a physical threshold, or a third-party observer—that interrupts the loop.

The debugging frame is valuable beyond its practical utility because it recontextualizes failure. When a system fails, the instinctive response is self-criticism—a judgment of the person rather than an analysis of the process. Debugging treats failure as a system property, not a character property. The question is not "why can't I follow through?" but "at which step did the algorithm diverge from its specification, and what modification will prevent the same divergence next time?" This is not merely a kindness. It is a more accurate model of how behavioral change actually works.

2.8 Algorithms for High-Stakes, Non-Recurring Decisions

The cases above involve recurring decisions—those that occur frequently enough to justify the investment of building a formal system. But algorithmic thinking also has a crucial application in genuinely novel, high-stakes situations where no prior template exists.

In these cases, the algorithm is not a pre-built routine but a **decision protocol**: a structured process for gathering information, evaluating options, and committing to a course of action that prevents the emotional hijacking and indefinite delay that characterize unstructured high-stakes deliberation.

A robust decision protocol for novel, significant choices has five stages.

Stage 1 – Scope Definition. Apply the Variable Audit from Chapter One. Establish S_0, S^*, variables, and constraints before any option evaluation begins. This stage prevents the common error of evaluating options against an undefined criterion.

Stage 2 – Option Generation. Generate at least three distinct options, including one that challenges your initial framing of the problem. The first option that comes to mind is usually the one most emotionally proximate, not the one most structurally sound. Forcing the generation of a third option after two have already been identified is a reliable technique for surfacing alternatives that the initial framing excluded.

Stage 3 – Criteria-Based Evaluation. For each option, evaluate performance on each of the decision criteria established in Stage 1. Assign scores or ranks where possible. The point is not to produce a mechanical verdict but to make the evaluation structure visible—so that the relative weight you place on different criteria can be examined and questioned rather than operating invisibly.

Stage 4 – Pre-Mortem. Before committing to the leading option, conduct a **pre-mortem**: imagine that it is twelve months from now and the choice has produced the worst plausible outcome. Working backward, what was the most likely cause? This technique, developed by psychologist Gary Klein, surfaces failure modes that optimism suppresses during forward-looking analysis. It is the algorithm's internal stress test.

Stage 5 – Commitment and Review Date. Make the decision, record it with a one-sentence rationale, and schedule a specific future date for review. The rationale serves as a baseline against which the review evaluates the quality of the reasoning, not just the quality of the outcome. A good process can produce a bad outcome through variance; a bad process can produce a good outcome through luck. Tracking the reasoning rather than just the result is how you distinguish between the two.

> *Decision Quality = Process Rigor × Information Completeness − Emotional Contamination*

2.9 Algorithmic Living Across Three Domains

Financial Algorithms

The most consequential single financial algorithm most people can build is a **spending trigger tree**. Rather than evaluating each purchase on its individual merits—a process dominated by in-the-moment desire and susceptible to post-hoc rationalization—a spending trigger tree establishes, in advance, the criteria that any non-recurring expenditure must meet before it is approved.

A basic version: Is this expenditure budgeted? If yes, proceed. If no: does it replace a critical failure? If yes, proceed with documentation. If no: does it exceed $100? If yes, apply the 48-hour rule—revisit in two days and re-evaluate. If no, approve. This simple tree eliminates the majority of impulse spending without requiring willpower at the moment of temptation. The algorithm resists on your behalf.

Productivity Algorithms

The most common failure mode in knowledge work is not insufficient effort but **insufficient sequencing**: tasks initiated in the wrong order, attention distributed across too many concurrent threads, reactive work displacing generative work. An algorithmic approach to the workday begins not with a task list but with a **task triage**: the daily classification of all pending work into four categories—Do Now (high urgency, high value), Schedule (high value, low urgency), Delegate (low value, doable by others), and Discard (low value, low urgency)—and the commitment to work through the categories in that order.

The algorithm also governs context-switching. Rather than allowing incoming messages and requests to interrupt the current task at will, a pre-committed communication algorithm—for example, checking messages at 9:00 am, 12:30 pm, and 4:00 pm only—removes the decision of when to check from each individual hour and consolidates communication costs into three bounded windows.

Interpersonal Algorithms

The most algorithmizable interpersonal situations are the ones that most reliably produce regret: responses sent in anger, commitments made under social pressure, conflicts escalated by reactive language. A communication algorithm for difficult conversations has a short execution sequence: identify the emotional state at trigger (if elevated, initiate a mandatory 60-minute delay); draft the response in writing before sending or speaking; read the draft against the question "does this address the actual problem or does it express my emotional reaction to the problem?"; revise if necessary; deliver.

The algorithm does not make the conversation easier. It makes it more likely to produce a useful outcome and less likely to produce an unnecessary escalation that requires its own subsequent repair.

2.10 The Deeper Promise of Algorithmic Living

There is a version of the argument in this chapter that can sound cold: reduce yourself to a set of rules, automate your responses, minimize deliberation. This reading misses the point entirely.

The purpose of building algorithms for recurring decisions is not to become mechanical. It is to **protect the space where genuine human judgment is irreplaceable.** Creative insight, moral reasoning, empathic response, adaptive strategy in genuinely novel situations—these capacities are not algorithmic, and they cannot be automated. But they are also profoundly vulnerable to the cognitive depletion produced by spending the same mental resources on what to have for lunch, whether to check the phone, and how to respond to the same type of difficult message for the fourteenth time.

Every algorithm you build for a recurring decision is a gift to your future self—a reduction in the cognitive tax that recurring decisions impose on the moments that matter most. The surgeon whose sterile field preparation is a flawless, automatic checklist does not bring less intelligence to the operating room. They bring *more*, because the algorithm has preserved their full attention for the decisions that no algorithm can make.

This is, ultimately, what it means to live algorithmically: not the removal of human agency, but the careful, deliberate *preservation* of it—for the problems worth the full weight of your most careful, most unencumbered thought.

Chapter Logic Check

☐ Which single recurring decision in my life currently consumes the most deliberation per execution—and can I write a decision tree that resolves it in advance?

☐ What is the trigger condition for my most consistent behavioral failure (overspending, over-committing, reactive communication)—and what three-step algorithm would intercept it before the failure occurs?

☐ Do I have a review gate scheduled for any of my existing systems, or are my current rules running on outdated criteria from a previous version of my circumstances?

Chapter 3

Thinking in Systems: Why Everything Is Connected to Everything Else

"You can never do merely one thing."
—Garrett Hardin

3.1 The Surgeon Who Fixed the Wrong Problem

In the early 1970s, a hospital in Vienna undertook a major initiative to reduce its surgical mortality rate. The administration identified a clear pattern in the data: deaths clustered in the weeks immediately following major operations, driven largely by post-surgical infections. The response was straightforward and locally rational—a rigorous new protocol for surgical suite sterilization, mandatory antibiotic regimens, and stricter wound care standards.

The protocols were implemented carefully. Compliance was high. And within eighteen months, post-surgical infection rates fell dramatically. The intervention, by every direct measure, had succeeded.

But the mortality rate did not improve.

What the administration had not anticipated was that the same population of patients who survived their surgeries due to reduced infections now required longer recovery stays, which increased bed occupancy, which increased waiting times for other surgical patients, which meant that patients with time-sensitive conditions were arriving at the operating table in worse condition than they would have six months earlier. The improvement in one part of the system had created a cascade of pressures elsewhere that offset it nearly entirely.

The surgical team had solved the problem they could see. They had missed the system that surrounded it.

This story is not exceptional. It is the default experience of anyone who attempts to improve a complex, interconnected situation by acting on a single isolated element—a company that cuts costs without examining what those costs were producing, a diet that restricts one nutrient without considering compensatory changes elsewhere in the diet, a policy designed to reduce one harm that inadvertently redistributes rather than eliminates it. The failure mode is consistent: intervening in a part without modeling the whole.

Systems thinking is the discipline of modeling the whole. It is the practice of seeing not just the element you intend to act on, but the relationships that connect it to every other element—and tracing, before you act, where the ripples will travel.

Chapter One taught you to define your problem precisely. Chapter Two taught you to build algorithms that solve it consistently. This chapter teaches you to map the *territory* those algorithms operate inside—because a precise problem statement and a well-built algorithm that fail to account for their systemic context will produce interventions as locally effective and globally self-defeating as the hospital's sterilization protocol.

3.2 What a System Is—and Is Not

The word "system" is used so broadly in ordinary language that it has nearly lost its technical meaning. People speak of "the system" meaning society, or "my system" meaning a personal habit, or "a broken system" meaning any institution they distrust. For the purposes of this chapter—and for the purposes of mathematical thinking more broadly—the term needs a precise definition.

A **system** is a set of elements connected by relationships that together produce a behavior that no individual element could produce alone.

Three components are essential, and all three must be present.

Elements are the visible, nameable parts: the people in an organization, the organs in a body, the accounts in a financial portfolio, the habits in a daily routine. Elements are the most natural entry point for analysis because they are concrete and enumerable. They are also, as the Vienna hospital discovered, the most dangerous part to focus on exclusively.

Relationships are the causal connections between elements: the rules, flows, signals, and dependencies that determine how a change in one element propagates to others. Relationships are often invisible in a casual inspection of a system. They do not show up on an organizational chart, a medical chart, or a budget spreadsheet. They must be inferred from behavior over time—from asking not "what does this element do?" but "how does a change in this element affect the behavior of everything connected to it?"

Function or purpose is what the system as a whole produces—the emergent behavior that arises from the interactions among its elements and relationships. This is the level at which systems most commonly surprise their inhabitants. The purpose of a system is not necessarily what its designers intended, nor what its participants claim. The purpose of a system is what it actually does, consistently, over time. An organization that claims to prioritize employee wellbeing but whose incentive structures consistently reward overwork has a system whose purpose is overwork, regardless of stated values. The system's behavior reveals its true purpose.

3.3 Stocks, Flows, and the Invisible Architecture of Change

The fundamental mathematical structure of any dynamic system is built from two primitives: **stocks** and **flows**.

A **stock** is an accumulation—the quantity of something present in the system at any given moment. Your savings account balance is a stock. Your physical fitness level is a stock. Your reputation in your industry is a stock. Your energy at the end of a workday is a stock. Stocks change slowly; they cannot jump instantly from one value to another. They are the memory of the system—the record of everything that has flowed in and out over time.

A **flow** is a rate of change that affects a stock over time. Your monthly savings rate is a flow into your savings stock. Your monthly expenses are a flow out of it. The physical training you do this week is a flow into your fitness stock;

sedentary behavior and aging are flows out of it. Flows are the mechanisms by which stocks change, and they are the primary levers available for deliberate intervention.

The relationship between stocks and flows is expressed in a form you may recognize from calculus:

$$S(t) = S(t_0) + \int_{t_0}^{t} \left[F_{\text{in}}(\tau) - F_{\text{out}}(\tau) \right] d\tau \qquad (3.1)$$

Where $S(t)$ is the stock value at time t, $S(t_0)$ is the initial value, and F_{in} and F_{out} are the inflow and outflow rates. Even if calculus is unfamiliar, the logic is accessible: the current value of any stock is its initial value plus everything that has flowed in, minus everything that has flowed out, from the beginning to now.

This formulation has immediate practical consequences.

Consequence 1: Stocks resist change. Because they represent accumulated history, stocks cannot be instantaneously modified regardless of how aggressively you intervene in the flows. You cannot become physically fit in a week regardless of how hard you train, because your fitness stock has decades of prior history built into its current value. You cannot repair a reputation in a month regardless of how impeccably you behave, because the stock reflects years of accumulated interactions. Impatience with the pace of change in stocks is one of the most common sources of discouragement in personal development—and it is almost always a consequence of misunderstanding the stock-flow structure rather than evidence that the effort is failing.

Consequence 2: Changing the flow changes the stock, eventually. The converse of Consequence 1 is equally important. Because the stock represents accumulated flows, any sustained change in a flow rate will, given sufficient time, produce a proportionally large change in the stock. A modest but persistent positive delta between inflows and outflows will build any stock dramatically over time. This is the systems-thinking foundation of what Chapter Six will describe as the law of compounding: the stock $S(t)$ grows not because any single inflow is large, but because the integral accumulates without interruption.

Consequence 3: To change a stock, you must change its flows—not the stock itself. This sounds obvious, but it is violated constantly in the way people attempt to change their lives. Trying to "feel more confident" is an attempt to change a stock directly, bypassing its flows. The intervention is not wrong; it is misdirected. The flow question is: what experiences, behaviors, or inputs consistently add to the confidence stock? Answering that question and engineering those inputs is the mechanistically correct intervention. The stock changes as a downstream consequence of sustained flow changes—not as a target of direct assault.

$$Stock(t) = Stock(t_0) + (Inflows - Outflows) \times Time$$

3.4 Feedback Loops: The Engine of System Behavior

Stocks and flows describe the structure of a system. **Feedback loops** describe its dynamics—the mechanisms by which a system's outputs circle back to influence its own inputs, creating self-regulating or self-amplifying behavior over time.

There are two fundamental types of feedback loop, and understanding the difference between them explains a vast range of otherwise puzzling real-world phenomena.

Reinforcing Loops (Positive Feedback)

A **reinforcing loop** is a self-amplifying cycle: a change in one direction produces effects that reinforce further change in the same direction. This is what most people mean by "momentum" or a "virtuous cycle"—or, in the negative direction, a "vicious cycle."

The mathematical signature of a reinforcing loop is exponential behavior. When you save money and the interest earned is reinvested, the interest itself earns interest, producing compounding growth. When you build a skill and the skill enables you to learn faster, the learning rate itself accelerates. When a city gains economic activity that makes it more attractive to businesses, which attract more workers, which create more economic activity, the reinforcing loop generates rapid concentration of growth.

The same structure runs in reverse. When a person feels increasingly behind on their work, the stress impairs focus, which reduces output, which creates more backlog, which increases stress. When a struggling business reduces staff to cut costs, the reduced capacity produces worse service, which reduces revenue, which forces further cost cuts. The feedback is identical in structure—a change producing effects that amplify the original change—regardless of whether the direction is desirable.

Balancing Loops (Negative Feedback)

A **balancing loop** is a self-correcting cycle: a change in one direction produces effects that resist or reverse that change, stabilizing the system around a target or equilibrium. Thermostats, homeostatic biological processes, and most market price mechanisms are balancing loops.

The mathematical signature of a balancing loop is goal-seeking behavior—the system "wants" to be at a particular state and generates corrective pressure whenever it deviates from it. Your body temperature is governed by dozens of interacting balancing loops that collectively maintain a narrow range around $37°C$ regardless of external conditions. A competitive market in which high prices attract new suppliers, which increases supply, which reduces prices, which stabilizes the market, is a balancing loop.

Balancing loops are not always benign. Any system with a goal that conflicts with what you want will produce balancing behavior that resists your intervention. An organization with a deep cultural norm around low risk-taking will generate social pressure that corrects toward conservatism every time a member attempts to introduce bold change, regardless of the explicit organizational mandate. A person with an unconscious "identity target" of being the struggling artist will generate subtle self-sabotage whenever circumstances push their income above that identity threshold. Understanding the balancing loop explains the resistance; targeting the loop's goal is the leverage point.

Mapping Your Loops

> *System Behavior = Structure of Feedback Loops +*
> *Time Delays*

The most immediately useful application of feedback loop analysis is the habit of asking, before any intervention: is this the result of a reinforcing loop or a balancing loop—and in which direction is it currently running?

A person whose health is deteriorating is experiencing either a reinforcing loop (one aspect of decline feeding another: poor sleep degrades diet choices, which degrade energy, which degrades exercise, which degrades sleep) or a balancing loop actively resisting improvement (a deeply held self-image as a sedentary person generating corrective pressure against each attempt to be otherwise). The two diagnoses call for different interventions. The reinforcing loop needs a circuit break—a targeted interruption at the element where the chain is most brittle. The balancing loop needs a *goal shift*—a change to the reference state the system is stabilizing toward, rather than a brute-force attempt to push the system past the resistance.

3.5 Time Delays: Why Obvious Interventions Produce Non-Obvious Results

Systems generate most of their surprising behavior not from their structure alone, but from the interaction of that structure with **time delays**—gaps between a cause and its effect that prevent the consequence of an action from being immediately visible.

Time delays are everywhere in complex systems. The link between dietary choices and cardiovascular health is separated by decades. The link between a management decision and its effect on organizational culture is separated by months or years. The link between a country's monetary policy and its inflation rate is separated by eighteen months to two years. The link between investing in a new skill and the career returns on that investment is separated by years of the Valley of Disappointment described in Chapter Six.

When time delays are long, two destructive patterns emerge.

Pattern 1: Over-correction. A policy is implemented, produces no visible result within the expected timeframe, is judged to have failed, and is reversed or replaced—just as the delayed consequence of the original policy is about to arrive. The reversal creates its own delayed consequence, which arrives after the next policy has been implemented and judged, producing an oscillation of interventions and counter-interventions that creates far more instability than the original problem. This pattern is recognizable in monetary policy, dietary fads, management restructuring cycles, and the alternating enthusiasm and abandonment of exercise routines.

Pattern 2: Accumulation blindness. Because the change in a stock happens slowly, and the flow rate producing it seems small in any single period, the growth is invisible until it is large. This is how debt accumulates to crisis, how a relationship erodes to rupture, how a professional skill gap grows to career threat, and—in the positive direction—how a consistent daily practice compounds to mastery. The same structure, the same delay, the same invisibility; the direction is the only difference.

The corrective for both patterns is the same: **extend your observational time horizon.** Evaluate your interventions not on their results in days or weeks but on their trajectory over months or quarters. The relevant question is not "is it working yet?" but "is the flow rate changing in the right direction?" If the flows are correct, the stock will follow. Patience with stocks is not passivity; it is systems literacy.

3.6 Emergence: When the Whole Becomes More Than Its Parts

One of the most intellectually important—and most practically consequential—properties of complex systems is **emergence**: the appearance of behaviors, properties, or capacities in a system as a whole that do not exist in any of its individual elements and cannot be predicted from an examination of those elements in isolation.

Consciousness emerges from the interaction of neurons, none of which are conscious. Market prices emerge from the interaction of buyers and sellers, none of whom individually determine price. The stability of an ecosystem emerges from the interaction of thousands of species, none of which individually constitute a stable system. Traffic jams emerge from the independent driving decisions of individual motorists, none of whom intended to create a jam.

Emergence is important for practical reasoning because it means that **analyzing a system's elements is not sufficient to understand the system's behavior.** The elements of a dysfunctional team may all be competent, well-intentioned individuals. The elements of a destructive habit loop may all be individually harmless behaviors. The elements of a financial crisis may all be institutions following locally rational rules. It is the *interactions*—the feedback loops, the time delays, the nonlinear relationships between elements—that produce the emergent behavior, for better or worse.

For the practical systems thinker, emergence carries a specific instruction: when a system is producing an outcome you did not intend and cannot explain by examining individual parts, look for interactions. Ask not "what is wrong with this element?" but "what is the feedback structure that is producing this behavior?" The locus of the problem is almost always in a relationship, not in a part.

3.7 Archetypes: The Recurring Patterns of System Failure

One of the most valuable contributions of systems thinking to practical reasoning is the identification of a small number of **system archetypes**—recurring structural patterns that appear across vastly different domains and produce predictably similar failure modes. Recognizing these archetypes in your own life is one of the highest-leverage applications of the material in this chapter.

The Limits to Growth Archetype

A reinforcing loop is driving growth or improvement, but at some point the growth encounters a constraint—a **limiting condition** that the growing element imposes on a system resource. If the constraint is not addressed, the growth slows, plateaus, or reverses—not because the reinforcing loop has stopped working, but because a balancing loop tied to the constraint is now dominating the system.

The pattern appears in: career trajectories that plateau when a skill bottleneck is reached; businesses that grow rapidly and then stall when management capacity cannot scale with demand; physical training programs that produce rapid initial gains followed by plateaus when recovery capacity becomes the limiting factor.

The counterintuitive prescription: do not push harder on the reinforcing loop. Identify and address the limiting condition. The leverage is in the constraint, not in the growth mechanism.

The Fixes That Fail Archetype

A problem symptom is addressed with an intervention that produces immediate relief but also generates a delayed side effect that worsens the original problem, creating dependency on the fix.

The pattern appears in: addressing fatigue with caffeine rather than sleep (the caffeine provides relief but degrades sleep quality, increasing underlying fatigue); addressing cash flow problems with debt (the debt provides relief but increases the interest burden, worsening the cash flow); addressing anxiety with avoidance (the avoidance provides relief but increases sensitivity to the avoided stimulus over time).

The prescription: trace the time-delayed side effect of your current fix and evaluate whether it is building or depleting the underlying stock the fix was designed to protect. If it is depleting, the fix is creating structural dependency rather than resolution.

The Tragedy of the Commons Archetype

Multiple actors share access to a common resource. Each actor's use of the resource is governed by individual self-interest, with the benefits of use accruing individually but the costs of depletion distributed across all actors. The individually rational behavior of each actor, aggregated, depletes the common resource at a rate that is collectively irrational.

The pattern appears in: shared office resources, team energy and attention (when everyone delegates more than they absorb), environmental commons, and the shared social infrastructure of trust (when individual actors defect from cooperative norms because others are doing so, depleting the overall cooperative capacity of the system).

The prescription: identify the shared resource, make the depletion rate visible to all actors, and establish a governance mechanism—a norm, a rule, a mutual accountability structure—that aligns individual incentives with collective sustainability.

3.8 Building Your System Map

The practical output of systems thinking is a **causal loop diagram**: a visual representation of the key stocks, flows, and feedback relationships in a specific domain of your life. You do not need specialized software or formal methodology to build a useful one. You need only the habit of asking two questions about any situation you are trying to understand or improve.

Question 1: What are the key stocks in this domain? Name the things that accumulate slowly over time and repre-

sent the current state of the system—the things you are trying
to build up or prevent from depleting. Write them down.

**Question 2: What are the feedback loops that con-
nect them?** For each stock, identify the primary inflows and
outflows, and then trace whether those flows are influenced
by the stock's own current level (a feedback relationship)
or by external factors. Label reinforcing loops with a + and
balancing loops with a —. Identify any significant time delays.

A completed causal loop diagram for, say, your professional development system might include stocks for skill level,
professional reputation, income, and time available for learning; flows driven by active study, applied practice, income-
generating work, and rest; reinforcing loops connecting skill
to reputation to income to capacity for investment in further
development; balancing loops connecting time allocation to
recovery; and time delays between skill acquisition and reputation change, and between reputation change and income
change.

This map will not tell you what to do. But it will tell
you where the leverage points are—the places in the system
where a small change in flows or goals would produce the
largest cumulative change in the stocks that matter most. And
leverage, as we will see in Chapter Four, is the only thing
worth optimizing.

3.9 Thinking in Systems Across Three Domains

Health as a System

The single most common failure in personal health is treating it as a collection of independent variables—diet, exercise,

sleep, stress—rather than as a tightly coupled system in which each element is both cause and consequence of the others. Sleep deprivation elevates cortisol, which increases appetite for calorie-dense food, which impairs recovery, which degrades exercise performance, which reduces the quality of subsequent sleep. The reinforcing loop runs in both directions: intervention at any single point that improves sleep quality also improves diet quality, exercise capacity, and stress regulation—not because those things are the same as sleep, but because the system connecting them is real, measurable, and responsive to deliberate management.

Finances as a System

The financial behaviors that most reliably predict long-term wealth are not the most dramatic ones—a large salary, a successful investment, a windfall. They are the ones that build and protect stocks over time through the structure of their flows: consistent saving rates that build capital stocks, expense structures that protect those flows from erosion, and diversified allocations that reduce the variance of the stock's trajectory. The financial system also contains dangerous archetypes: the Fixes That Fail pattern appears in every cycle of debt-funded consumption; the Limits to Growth pattern appears in every income plateau caused by an unaddressed skill constraint.

Relationships as a System

Every significant long-term relationship is a system with identifiable stocks (trust, goodwill, shared history, emotional safety), flows (interactions, acts of repair, withdrawals under stress), and feedback loops (the 5:1 stability ratio from Chapter Eight is a reinforcing loop: positive interactions make the relationship more resilient, which makes positive interactions easier and more likely). The most important time delay in relationship systems is the delay between a pattern of behavior and its effect on the trust stock—the reason that by the time a relationship's dysfunction is obvious, the underlying stock has often been depleted for much longer than either party recognized.

3.10 The Discipline of Second-Order Attention

The systems thinking framework asks you to hold two levels of attention simultaneously: the immediate, visible level of events and actions, and the deeper, structural level of stocks, flows, and feedback relationships that generate those events over time.

In Donella Meadows's foundational work on systems thinking, she described the hierarchy of leverage points in a system—ordered from weakest to most powerful. At the weak end: changing parameters (adjusting numbers within an existing structure). Moving higher: changing the rules, changing the information flows, changing the goals of subsystems. At the most powerful end: changing the mindset or paradigm out of which the entire system arises.

This hierarchy has a practical corollary: the interventions that feel most direct—changing a behavior, adjusting a number—are usually at the low end of the leverage hierarchy. The interventions that feel most abstract—questioning an assumption, restructuring a feedback relationship, reframing the goal—are usually at the high end. The most powerful place to intervene in a system is almost never where the problem is most visible.

This is the deepest contribution of systems thinking to mathematical living. It does not merely add tools to your problem-solving toolkit. It changes the level at which you engage with problems—elevating your attention from "what happened?" to "what structure produced this, and what change to that structure would produce something different?"

When you see a recurring problem, the systems thinker's first question is not "what do I do about this?" It is: "what feedback loop is generating this, how long has it been running, and where is the leverage point that would change its direction?"

The answer to that question is almost never obvious. But it is almost always available—to anyone willing to look at the system rather than just at the parts.

Chapter Logic Check

- [ ] In my most important current challenge, what are the key *stocks*—the things that accumulate slowly and represent the underlying health of the system—and am I tracking them, or only reacting to visible events?

- [ ] What reinforcing loop is most responsible for the best trajectory currently in my life—and what is the single input that, if disrupted, would break the loop?

- [ ] Where in my life am I applying a "fix" that provides short-term relief but has a time-delayed side effect that is quietly depleting the stock it was designed to protect?

Chapter 4

The Calculus of Tradeoffs: The Power of Constraints

"The essence of strategy is choosing what not to do."
—Michael Porter

4.1 The Inconsistent System

There is a certain kind of person who seems to have made a commitment to accomplish everything. They will reach the top of their field and be fully present at home. They will maintain elite physical fitness and get eight hours of sleep. They will build a thriving social life, pursue creative projects, serve their community, read seriously, and travel widely—all simultaneously, indefinitely, without apparent sacrifice.

You have almost certainly encountered this person in the form of aspirational content: the early-morning ritual of the executive who also finds time to journal, meditate, train for a marathon, cook whole foods from scratch, and mentor junior colleagues before the rest of the world has finished its first cup of coffee. The implicit message is that time is not actually zero-sum—that with sufficient discipline and optimization, the constraints that govern ordinary lives can be transcended.

This message is mathematically false.

In linear algebra, a system of equations is called **consistent** if it has at least one solution, and **inconsistent** if it has none. An inconsistent system is not a hard system. It is not a system that requires more effort or creativity to solve. It is a system that has no solution by definition, regardless of the solver's talent or determination.

The list of simultaneous maximizations described above is an inconsistent system. It cannot be solved. It can only be performed—temporarily, at high cost, until the hidden tradeoffs reassert themselves in the form of burnout, injury, relational damage, or the quiet collapse of whichever variable was being secretly sacrificed to maintain the appearance of all others.

The mathematics of constraints is not pessimistic. It is liberating. Once you accept that tradeoffs are not failures of optimization but structural features of any real system, you can stop trying to escape them and start making them deliberately. The person who consciously chooses which variables to maximize, and which to hold at minimum viable levels, is not doing less than the person who claims to maximize everything. They are doing something incomparably more sophisticated: they are solving the right problem.

4.2 The Zero-Sum Reality of Time

The most fundamental and least negotiable constraint in any human life is time. Not energy, not money, not motivation—time. Every other resource can be replenished, borrowed, or substituted. Time cannot. The twenty-four hours available to you today are the twenty-four hours available to the most productive person who has ever lived. The constraint is universal and absolute.

In physics, the Law of Conservation of Energy establishes that the total energy in a closed system is constant. Energy cannot be created from nothing; it can only be transformed from one form to another. Time follows an analogous conservation principle:

$$T_{\text{total}} = T_{\text{work}} + T_{\text{rest}} + T_{\text{leisure}} + T_{\text{maintenance}} \qquad (4.1)$$

Where $T_{\text{maintenance}}$ represents the irreducible overhead of biological existence—sleep, eating, hygiene, transit. This term is not optional. It is a hard constant that, when subtracted from $T_{\text{total}} = 24$, reveals the true discretionary time available for the other variables.

For most adults, $T_{\text{maintenance}}$ consumes approximately 8–10 hours per day when sleep is included honestly. This leaves 14–16 hours in which T_{work} and T_{leisure} must coexist. If T_{work} averages 10 hours, T_{leisure} averages 4–6. Within that leisure window, every commitment—family, fitness, social life, creative pursuits, rest—must be accommodated.

This is not a depressing calculation. It is an honest one. And honest calculations are the only kind that produce useful plans.

The refusal to acknowledge the time constraint takes two forms, both destructive.

The first is **optimism bias**: the belief that the schedule will be more available in the future than it is today. Next month will be less busy. After this project, there will be more time. The constraint is real now but will loosen later. This belief is almost never accurate—periods of relative availability tend to be filled with new commitments as automatically as a vacuum fills with air—and it functions as a permanent deferral of any serious engagement with time as a finite resource.

The second is **accounting fraud**: maintaining the pretense that all commitments are being honored while silently running a deficit in one or more of the variables. The sleep variable is the most common victim—reduced gradually, in increments too small to feel decisive, until the accumulated deficit produces cognitive impairment that is never attributed to its actual cause. The rest and leisure variables follow. The system does not fail visibly; it degrades silently, and the person experiencing the degradation frequently attributes it to character failure—lack of discipline, insufficient resilience—rather than to a time equation that has been running in deficit for months.

The corrective is to do the arithmetic. Write down your actual weekly time allocation across all categories. Sum the columns. Compare to 168 hours. The gap between what is claimed and what is arithmetically possible is the measure of the hidden deficit currently being charged against some unstated variable.

4.3 The Production Possibility Frontier

The **Production Possibility Frontier** (PPF) is one of economics' most elegant and most broadly applicable concepts. Developed to describe the output tradeoffs between two goods in a fixed-resource economy, it applies with equal precision to any situation in which a fixed resource must be allocated between competing uses.

The PPF for a life with two primary outputs—professional achievement and personal wellbeing—is a curve in two-dimensional space. Every point on the curve represents a fully efficient allocation: all available resources are deployed, none are wasted, and the only way to increase one output is to decrease the other. Points inside the curve represent inefficiency: resources are being wasted, and it is possible to increase both outputs simultaneously by eliminating the waste. Points outside the curve are infeasible: they exceed what the fixed resource endowment makes possible.

$$Opportunity\ Cost = Value_{Foregone} - Value_{Chosen}$$

The PPF makes the concept of **opportunity cost** geometrically visible. Moving along the frontier from one point to another—trading professional output for personal wellbeing, or vice versa—has a slope at every point. That slope is the opportunity cost: the units of one output that must be surrendered for each additional unit of the other.

The slope is not constant. At the extremes of specialization—when nearly all resources are devoted to one output—the marginal opportunity cost of further specialization rises steeply. The first hour removed from professional output to invest in personal wellbeing produces a large gain in the latter and a small loss in the former. The tenth such hour produces a smaller gain and a larger loss. This is the principle of **increasing marginal costs of specialization**, and it is why extreme focus in any single domain eventually becomes self-defeating.

In practical terms: the PPF argues for a portfolio approach to life priorities rather than a monomaniacal one. The mathematically optimal allocation is almost never the corner solution that maximizes one variable to the exclusion of all others. It is an interior point on the frontier—one that balances across dimensions in proportion to their relative marginal values. The question is not "should I prioritize work or life?" but "where on the frontier does my current allocation sit, and in which direction does moving along it produce the greatest net value?"

4.4 Opportunity Cost: The Price of Invisible Alternatives

The concept of opportunity cost is among the most consistently underweighted factors in human decision-making. This is not a character failing; it is a consequence of the way attention works. The option you choose is visible, concrete, and present. The option you forgo is invisible, hypothetical, and absent. The brain assigns dramatically more weight to what it can see than to what it must infer.

Every allocation of a finite resource—time, money, attention, energy—has an opportunity cost equal to the value of the best alternative use of that resource. This cost is real regardless of whether it is calculated. The person who spends Saturday afternoon watching television does not merely receive the value (or non-value) of television. They also pay the cost of whatever else Saturday afternoon could have produced: rest, exercise, a meaningful conversation, progress on a project, quality time with a child.

$$\text{True Cost of Action } A = \text{Direct Cost}(A) + \text{Opportunity Cost}(A) \tag{4.2}$$

The direct cost is what you see on the receipt. The opportunity cost is the receipt you never receive—from the alternative reality in which you made a different choice. Both are real. Only one shows up in most people's accounting.

The practical discipline of opportunity cost thinking is to name the alternative before committing to the choice. Not as a hedge or a source of regret, but as part of the decision calculus. Before saying yes to a commitment, ask: what is the best use of this same resource that I am declining in order to say yes? If the answer is something genuinely less valuable than the commitment being accepted, proceed without reservation. If the answer is something more valuable—or unknown—the decision deserves more examination.

4.5 The Theory of Constraints: Finding Your Bottleneck

In manufacturing operations research, the **Theory of Constraints** addresses a phenomenon that seems counterintuitive until you have seen it: in any complex system with multiple interdependent processes, the overall output of the system is determined entirely by the single slowest step—the **bottleneck**—regardless of the speed or efficiency of every other step.

Eliyahu Goldratt formalized this observation into a management methodology in his 1984 book *The Goal*. The core demonstration: a factory with a production chain of ten steps, nine of which can process one thousand units per hour and one of which can process only ten, produces ten units per hour. The nine efficient steps produce no advantage because their output cannot be absorbed by the bottleneck. All capacity upstream of the bottleneck generates work-in-progress inventory that accumulates without contributing to throughput. All capacity downstream of the bottleneck sits idle, waiting for the bottleneck to release its constrained output.

The prescription is a five-step process:

1. **Identify** the constraint: which single element is limiting the system's output?

2. **Exploit** the constraint: ensure the limiting element operates at maximum capacity. Remove anything that causes it to be idle.

3. **Subordinate** everything else: configure all non-constraining elements to support the constraint's maximum utilization, not their own.

4. **Elevate** the constraint: invest in increasing the capacity of the bottleneck—but only after it has been fully exploited.

5. **Repeat**: once the bottleneck has been elevated, a new constraint will emerge elsewhere in the system. Return to step one.

The Theory of Constraints applied to personal productivity reveals a pathology that is nearly universal: people optimize non-constraints. They spend their most careful attention on tasks and systems that are not limiting their overall output, while the actual bottleneck continues to throttle the system at its constrained rate.

The most common personal bottlenecks are not what people typically identify when asked. They are rarely the obvious inputs—hours worked, access to information, raw effort. The most common bottlenecks are subtler: **decision latency** (the time between recognizing what needs to be done and actually beginning it); **context quality** (the clarity and organization of the environment in which focused work happens); **recovery capacity** (the ability to restore cognitive function between high-demand periods); and **skill gaps** in a specific technical domain that is on the critical path of every meaningful project.

> *System Output $\leq$ Capacity of the Weakest Constraint*

Identifying your actual bottleneck requires the same honest measurement discipline as the Variable Audit from Chapter One. The question is not "where am I working hardest?" but "where, if I removed the constraint, would my overall output increase most?" These questions have different answers in most people's lives, and the gap between them represents the energy currently being spent on non-constraint optimization.

4.6 The Counterintuitive Gift of Constraints

There is a common and understandable response to the material in this chapter: constraint as limit, as ceiling, as evidence of insufficiency. If your time is bounded and your attention is finite and your bottleneck throttles your output, the feeling can be one of confinement—a universe smaller than ambition requires.

This reading is backwards.

In mathematics, an **unconstrained optimization** problem—one in which no limits are imposed on the variables—almost always has a trivial or degenerate solution. The unconstrained maximum of most objective functions is either infinity (which is not achievable) or a boundary solution that provides no useful information. It is the constraints that create the interesting structure of the problem. They bound the feasible region, create nontrivial tradeoffs, and force solutions that are genuinely optimal in the space of what is achievable rather than merely the direction of most desire.

The constraint that says you have 168 hours per week is not an obstacle to a good life. It is the structure that makes a good life designable. Without it, "a good life" would have no shape, no prioritization, no defined frontier against which choices could be evaluated. The constraint forces the question: given finite resources, what allocation produces the most value? And that question, once honestly engaged, produces answers that are far more useful than the pseudo-answers produced by pretending the constraints do not exist.

Poets understand this intuitively. The sonnet's fourteen lines and strict rhyme scheme are not limitations on expression; they are the structure that gives the form its power. The haiku's seventeen syllables create a compression that produces insight unavailable in unconstrained prose. The constraint is the generator of form, and form is the carrier of meaning.

Your constraints—the irreducible $T_{\text{maintenance}}$, the finite attention span, the limited capital, the genuine bottleneck in your most important system—are not the enemies of your ambitions. They are the coordinates of the space in which your ambitions must live. Map them accurately, and you can navigate deliberately. Ignore them, and you will navigate by fantasy until reality reasserts itself, usually at considerable cost.

4.7 Making Tradeoffs Consciously: The Priority Stack

The practical tool for translating the theory of this chapter into daily decision-making is the **Priority Stack**: an explicit, ordered ranking of the variables you are choosing to optimize, together with the minimum acceptable levels for the variables you are choosing not to prioritize.

A priority stack has three tiers.

Tier 1: The Optimization Target. The single variable you are choosing to maximize in the current period. Not a list; a single variable. The PPF argument applies: attempting to simultaneously maximize more than one variable drives you toward the interior of the frontier, where every resource decision is compromised by the competing demands. Nominate one thing. Everything else becomes a constraint on that choice, not a co-equal objective.

Tier 2: The Threshold Variables. The other domains of life that matter but are not currently the optimization target. For each, specify the *minimum acceptable level*—the floor below which you will not allow them to fall, regardless of the demands of the Tier 1 optimization. The thresholds are set by your values, not by what is convenient for the optimization. Sleep is a threshold for most people: below seven hours, cognitive function declines in ways that impair the Tier 1 optimization itself, making the tradeoff self-defeating. Key relationships are thresholds. Physical health sufficient to sustain function is a threshold.

Tier 3: The Conscious Deferral. The things you genuinely care about that you are choosing not to engage with during this period. Not abandoned—deferred, with a specified future date for reassessment. The act of explicit deferral is important because it converts "I don't have time for this" from a passive frustration into a deliberate choice. Choices can be reconsidered at defined points; passive frustrations simply accumulate.

The priority stack is not a permanent document. It is a periodic one, reviewed at the same rhythm as the review gates in Chapter Two. Circumstances change, the Tier 1 optimization is achieved or abandoned, thresholds are renegotiated. The stack is a snapshot of your current best answer to the allocation problem, not a lifetime commitment.

4.8 The Mathematics of "No"

Among the practical applications of constraint thinking, none is more immediately impactful than the capacity to decline commitments that fall outside the priority stack with clear, mathematical reasoning rather than apology or excuse.

Most people experience the word "no" as a social failure—a disappointment of expectations, a withdrawal of goodwill, an admission of limitation. This experience is a consequence of framing the rejection in personal terms. "I can't do that" implies incapacity. "I don't want to do that" implies indifference. Both carry social cost.

The reframe that constraint thinking provides is mathematical rather than personal. The correct response to a request that falls outside the priority stack is not "I can't" or "I don't want to." It is: "I have a fixed resource that I have allocated to specific priorities, and accepting this would require displacing one of them. Given the current priority stack, I cannot accept without sacrificing something more important."

This is not a refusal based on capacity or desire. It is a refusal based on optimization. The constraint is the allocation, not the person. Framed this way, the "no" carries none of the social weight of personal rejection—it is the mathematical consequence of a finite resource already deployed.

The deeper effect of this reframe is internal as much as external. A person who understands their constraints as a priority structure rather than a set of limitations makes peace with the tradeoffs they are choosing instead of experiencing them as deprivations. The time not spent on the deferred interest is not time wasted or withheld; it is time allocated to the current optimization target. The difference in emotional experience—between deprivation and deliberate choice—is substantial and sustained.

4.9 The 168-Hour Audit: Doing the Arithmetic Honestly

Abstract acknowledgment of the time constraint is not the same as confronting it numerically. Most people have a vague sense that they are busy and that their schedule is full, but have never actually tabulated their 168 weekly hours with the same rigor they would bring to a financial budget. The exercise is uncomfortable, revealing, and essential.

The 168-hour audit proceeds in three stages.

Stage 1: Fixed costs. Begin with the irreducible time costs of biological existence: sleep (ideally 7–9 hours per night, meaning 49–63 hours per week), eating and meal preparation (estimate honestly, including all incidental consumption), personal hygiene and maintenance, and commuting. For most adults, these fixed costs total between 70 and 85 hours per week. Subtracting from 168 leaves a true discretionary pool of 83–98 hours.

Stage 2: Committed time. Next, account for non-optional obligations: employed work hours, contractual commitments, caregiving responsibilities, standing appointments. These vary enormously by life stage and circumstance. A parent of young children and a childless professional in the same job may have discretionary pools that differ by 20–30 hours per week—not because one is more disciplined, but because their constraint sets are categorically different. The audit makes this visible rather than allowing the difference to produce vague guilt on both sides.

Stage 3: Elective allocation. The remainder—typically 10–30 hours for most working adults, sometimes less—is the pool from which all non-obligatory life activities are funded: exercise, relationships, creative work, education, rest, and leisure. Mapping how this pool is actually being spent, versus how you believe it is being spent, is frequently the most instructive part of the exercise. Most people discover significant gaps between intention and actuality, and most of those gaps flow in the same direction: discretionary time is being consumed by low-priority activities that have never been deliberately chosen, while higher-priority activities are chronically underfunded.

The audit produces a number that cannot be argued with: the gap between the hours required to pursue your stated priorities at the level of effort they deserve, and the hours actually available after existing commitments. If the gap is positive—if there are more available hours than required—you have a resource deployment problem, not a constraint problem. If the gap is negative—more required than available—you have a genuine constraint, and the only rational responses are eliminating a committed obligation, degrading the execution standard of a lower-priority activity, or revising the ambition of the stated priority.

$$H_{\text{discretionary}} = 168 - H_{\text{biological}} - H_{\text{committed}} \qquad (4.3)$$

What the audit most reliably reveals is not scarcity but **misallocation**. Time that is nominally available is frequently colonized by activities that are neither enjoyable enough to defend as leisure nor productive enough to defend as work—the passive consumption of media, the reflexive checking of communication channels, the half-committed engagement with tasks that is neither rest nor progress. Eliminating or reducing these activities recovers the discretionary hours that better-aligned priorities require, without requiring any reduction in the fixed costs or committed obligations.

4.10 Tradeoffs Across Life Phases

One of the most liberating insights the constraint framework provides is that the optimal allocation changes across life phases—and that an allocation optimized for one phase may be entirely wrong for another. The tradeoffs are not permanent; they are the current solution to the current version of the optimization problem.

In the early career phase, the dominant constraint is typically skill and reputation capital. The PPF at this stage rewards heavy investment in learning, even at the cost of near-term financial return or work-life balance. The opportunity cost of not developing foundational skills in this phase is high because the compounding runway is long; each year of early skill investment generates decades of subsequent return. The appropriate optimization target for many people in this phase is *learning rate,* and the threshold variables are the minimum standards of health and relationship maintenance that sustain that rate.

In the family formation phase, the dominant constraint shifts. Time becomes the binding resource rather than the development capital that the early career phase required. The PPF is fundamentally different: the marginal value of additional professional time investment declines (because the foundational skills are largely built) while the marginal value of relational investment rises (because the compounding stock of family connection is being laid during a uniquely sensitive window). The optimization target and threshold structure that was correct in the previous phase may be structurally wrong here.

In later life phases, the constraint set shifts again—toward energy, toward the preservation of optionality, toward the harvest of the reputation and relationship stocks built in earlier phases. The person who applies early-career time-maximization logic to a later-career phase is running an outdated algorithm on a changed system. The constraint math has changed. The optimization should change with it.

Understanding your current life phase—and the specific constraint structure it implies—is not fatalistic. It is the precondition for designing an allocation that is genuinely optimal for this phase rather than borrowed from a phase that has passed or anticipated too early.

Chapter Logic Check

☐ When I write down my actual time allocation across all categories this week, does the arithmetic balance to 168 hours—and if not, which variable is running the hidden deficit?

☐ What is my current Tier 1 optimization target, and which commitments am I currently maintaining that are not supporting it and are not protecting a genuine threshold?

☐ Where in my most important system is the true bottleneck—and am I currently investing my most careful attention in exploiting it, or in improving something that is not on the critical path?

Chapter 5

Probabilities Over Emotions: Managing Risk

"The most important thing is to be able to think clearly without emotions getting in the way."
—Michael Lewis, *The Undoing Project*

5.1 The Statistician You Were Never Meant to Be

Evolution is the most successful optimization process in the history of the known universe, but it optimizes for reproductive fitness in the ancestral environment—not for rational decision-making in the twenty-first century. The human brain that navigates modern financial decisions, career choices, and social commitments is the same brain that spent the vast majority of its evolutionary history managing immediate, concrete, physical threats: predators, rivals, starvation, exclusion from the group. For these threats, emotional decision-making is highly effective. The fear response is fast, visceral, and calibrated to produce rapid physical action. The social belonging response is sensitive, persistent, and calibrated to prevent the kind of group exclusion that was, in evolutionary terms, tantamount to a death sentence.

The problem is that modern decisions are almost never immediate, concrete, or physical. They are probabilistic, multi-period, and abstract. The anxiety produced by a volatile investment portfolio is experienced by the brain in essentially the same registers as the anxiety produced by a predator—but the correct response to a predator (flee or fight, immediately) is precisely the wrong response to a volatile portfolio (stay the course, don't act). The social pain of a negative performance review is experienced in essentially the same registers as the social pain of group rejection—but the correct response to rejection (repair social bonds, signal conformity) may be precisely the wrong response to a bad review (advocate for your perspective, request a reassessment).

The gap between the emotional responses we were built for and the probabilistic decisions we actually face is the source of a predictable and well-documented set of cognitive errors. Understanding these errors is not an exercise in self-criticism. It is diagnostic preparation: if you know where the system fails, you can design compensating algorithms—exactly as Chapter Two suggested—that intercept the failure before it produces a decision you will regret.

5.2 The Taxonomy of Cognitive Bias: Where Emotion Hijacks the Equation

Since the foundational work of Daniel Kahneman and Amos Tversky in the 1970s and 1980s, cognitive scientists have cat-alogued dozens of systematic biases in human probabilistic reasoning. For the purposes of this chapter, four deserve par-ticular attention because they are the most consequential in everyday financial, professional, and interpersonal decisions.

Loss Aversion

In a landmark series of experiments, Kahneman and Tversky established that the subjective pain of losing a sum of money is approximately twice as powerful as the subjective pleasure of gaining the same amount. The finding has been replicated across cultures, income levels, and types of loss.

The practical consequence is a systematic bias away from positive-expected-value actions when those actions involve risk of loss, even when the probability structure clearly favors taking them. An investor who refuses to hold a portfolio with a 10% annual probability of a 15% drawdown, despite that portfolio having an expected annual return of 12%, is making a loss-aversion error: the emotional weight assigned to the potential loss exceeds what the math justifies.

Availability Heuristic

The ease with which an event can be recalled or imagined serves as a powerful proxy for its perceived probability. Events that are vivid, recent, emotionally charged, or heavily covered by media are judged to be more likely than events that are equally or more probable but less cognitively available.

The plane crash you read about last week makes flying feel more dangerous than driving, despite the statistical risk being orders of magnitude lower. The dramatic startup success story in last month's magazine makes entrepreneurship feel more reliably rewarding than the base-rate data justifies. The availability heuristic inflates the perceived probability of salient events and deflates the perceived probability of common but undramatic ones.

Overconfidence Bias

The research on calibration—the alignment between stated confidence levels and actual accuracy rates—is among the most robust and most humbling in cognitive psychology. When people say they are "90% confident" in a claim, they are typically correct far less than 90% of the time. Experts are not immune; in many studies, domain expertise increases overconfidence rather than reducing it, because expertise increases fluency of retrieval, and fluency is (incorrectly) experienced as accuracy.

For practical decision-making, overconfidence produces two failure modes: underestimation of the probability of adverse outcomes ("I'm sure this project will be done on time") and underestimation of the variance around expected outcomes ("I expect this investment to return 15%, give or take 2%" when the actual give or take is 20%).

Sunk Cost Fallacy

Resources already expended cannot be recovered regardless of future decisions. The rational criterion for any forward-looking decision is the expected value of future outcomes, which is entirely independent of past expenditures. The sunk cost fallacy is the persistent tendency to allow past expenditures to influence forward-looking decisions—to continue a failing project because of how much has already been invested, to remain in a deteriorating situation because of the time already committed, to hold a declining asset because of the price originally paid.

The sunk cost is not relevant to the decision. The question is always: given the current state of the world, what is

the expected value of each available option from this point
forward? The history of how you arrived at the current state
is context, not input.

5.3 The Expected Value Decider

Against this background of documented failure modes, the **Expected Value** framework provides a compensating structure.
It does not eliminate emotion from decision-making—nor
should it; emotion carries genuine information about prefer-
ences and values that pure calculation cannot capture. What
it does is give the analytical system a formal procedure that
can be run alongside the emotional response, providing a
check against the systematic biases described above.

$$EV = \left(P_{\text{win}} \times V_{\text{win}}\right) - \left(P_{\text{loss}} \times C_{\text{loss}}\right) \qquad (5.1)$$

Where:

- P_{win}: The probability of the favorable outcome, estimated as rigorously as available evidence allows.

- V_{win}: The value of the favorable outcome, including
  delayed and indirect benefits.

- P_{loss}: The probability of the adverse outcome ($1 - P_{\text{win}}$
  for a binary decision).

- C_{loss}: The cost of the adverse outcome, including delayed and indirect costs.

A decision with positive EV is, on average, beneficial to
take. A decision with negative EV is, on average, harmful
to take. The calculation does not guarantee any particular

outcome on any individual trial—variance ensures that even correct decisions produce bad results some fraction of the time—but it does guarantee that over a sufficient number of decisions, a policy of accepting positive-EV choices and declining negative-EV ones will produce better results than the alternative.

The discipline of the EV calculation is not primarily in the arithmetic. It is in the forced precision it demands at each step. Estimating P_{win} requires you to confront the probability of failure rather than letting optimism bias treat success as the default. Estimating C_{loss} requires you to quantify the downside rather than letting loss aversion inflate it beyond its true magnitude. Writing these numbers down—even approximately—has a stabilizing effect that the vague sense of "maybe it'll work" does not.

5.4 Calibration: The Art of Knowing What You Don't Know

The EV framework is only as good as the probability estimates fed into it. A decision made with a dramatically miscalibrated P_{win} is not better than a purely emotional decision; it is an emotional decision dressed in mathematical clothing, which may in fact be worse because it carries false authority.

Calibration is the alignment between stated confidence and actual accuracy: a perfectly calibrated forecaster who assigns 70% probability to an event should see that event occur 70% of the time across all the forecasts they have assigned 70% probability. Not on any single forecast—but aggregated across many.

The research on calibration by Philip Tetlock and colleagues, compiled in *Superforecasting*, identified the cognitive habits that distinguish well-calibrated forecasters ("superforecasters") from poorly calibrated ones. The distinguishing habits are not extraordinary intelligence or domain expertise. They are:

1. **Reference class forecasting:** Before estimating the probability of a specific outcome, identify the relevant reference class of similar situations and consult the base rate. How often do projects of this type, in this domain, at this stage, succeed? The base rate is your prior. Adjust from there, but anchor to it.

2. **Granularity:** Use specific probability values (63%, 71%) rather than vague categories ("likely," "probably"). Forcing granularity prevents the deliberate vagueness that allows forecasts to be interpreted as accurate regardless of what happens.

3. **Actively considering the opposing case:** Before finalizing a probability estimate, dedicate deliberate effort to the scenario in which you are wrong. What is the argument for the alternative outcome? What evidence would look exactly the same in both the world where you are right and the world where you are wrong?

4. **Tracking and updating:** Keep a record of forecasts and outcomes. Review your calibration periodically. If your 80% confidence events are actually occurring 60% of the time, you are systematically overconfident and should adjust.

The last point is the most uncomfortable and the most valuable. Calibration cannot be improved without feedback, and feedback requires maintaining a record that makes your errors visible to you. Most people avoid this because the record is humbling. But the humbling is the mechanism—it is the data that allows the mental model to be revised, which is the entire point.

> *Good Decision = Positive EV + Well-Calibrated P*
> *+ Accounted Variance*

5.5 Variance: The Correct Interpretation of Bad Outcomes

Even a mathematically optimal decision—positive EV, well-calibrated probabilities, full accounting of costs—will produce a bad outcome some fraction of the time. This is not a defect of the method. It is the honest mathematics of probability. In any system governed by probabilistic laws, the outcome of a single trial is not a reliable indicator of the quality of the process that produced it.

In statistics, **variance** is the measure of dispersion in a distribution of outcomes. A low-variance process produces outcomes that cluster closely around the expected value. A high-variance process produces outcomes spread widely around it. The critical insight is that the same expected value can be achieved by processes with very different variances—and that variance is not failure. It is uncertainty quantified.

$$\text{Outcome} = \text{Skill (Process)} + \text{Variance (Luck)} \qquad (5.2)$$

This decomposition has profound implications for how you should interpret both your successes and your failures.

A success produced primarily by variance—a high-variance decision that happened to land favorably—should not be attributed to the quality of the process. It should be recognized as fortunate and examined carefully before being replicated. A failure produced primarily by variance—a positive-EV decision that landed in the unfavorable tail—should not be attributed to the failure of the process. It should be recognized as the expected behavior of a well-designed system encountering its inherent uncertainty.

Most people do the opposite. They attribute successes to their own judgment and failures to bad luck—a well-documented bias called the **self-serving attribution error**. The mathematical reversal is more honest and more instructive: evaluate the process, not the outcome. Ask not "did this work?" but "was this a positive-EV decision given what was known at the time?" If yes, the process was correct regardless of the outcome. If no, the process was flawed regardless of whether it happened to produce a good result.

This distinction matters practically because it determines what you repeat. If you repeat processes that happened to produce good outcomes regardless of their quality, you accumulate variance risk without accumulated edge. If you repeat processes that are genuinely positive-EV, the variance averages out over time in your favor. The long run is kind to good processes and indifferent to lucky ones.

5.6 Bayesian Updating: The Logic of New Evidence

The Expected Value framework establishes how to evaluate decisions under a given probability estimate. Bayesian reasoning addresses the prior question: how should the estimate itself change as new evidence arrives?

Bayes' Theorem is the mathematical rule for updating the probability of a hypothesis in response to new data:

$$P(H \mid D) = \frac{P(D \mid H)\,P(H)}{P(D)} \qquad (5.3)$$

Where:

- $P(H)$: The **prior** probability of the hypothesis before observing the data.

- $P(D \mid H)$: The **likelihood**—how probable the observed data would be if the hypothesis were true.

- $P(D)$: The **marginal likelihood**—how probable the observed data is across all possible hypotheses.

- $P(H \mid D)$: The **posterior**—the updated probability of the hypothesis given the data.

In plain terms: you start with a prior belief about the probability of something. You observe new evidence. You update your belief in proportion to how strongly that evidence distinguishes the hypothesis from its alternatives. The posterior becomes the prior for the next update.

The Bayesian framework has two properties that directly counteract the cognitive biases described earlier. First, it formally requires the prior to be stated before the data is examined—preventing the post-hoc rationalization that allows people to claim they "always expected" the outcome that actually occurred. Second, it explicitly models the degree of update that evidence justifies—preventing both the over-updating that characterizes availability heuristic thinking and the under-updating that characterizes confirmation bias.

In practical life, Bayesian updating means that when a business partner misses a deadline, a friend cancels plans at the last minute, or an investment thesis fails to materialize on schedule, the appropriate response is not emotional reaction but **systematic revision**. The event is data. The question is: how much should this data change my probability estimate of the relevant hypothesis? If the partner's reliability prior was 90% and they have now missed one deadline in ten commitments, the posterior reliability estimate might be 85%—meaningfully lower, but not the catastrophic collapse that an emotionally driven reassessment might produce. If they have missed five deadlines in ten commitments, the posterior might be 55%—a fundamentally different working relationship warranted.

The Bayesian frame also prevents the opposite error: insufficient updating. A person who absorbs multiple pieces of confirming evidence for a flawed belief without appropriately revising upward the probability of the alternative is not being consistent—they are applying confirmation bias. Bayesian reasoning requires updating in both directions: increasing the probability of hypotheses supported by evidence and decreasing the probability of those contradicted by it.

5.7 Risk Versus Uncertainty: Knowing What You Don't Know

The economist Frank Knight drew a distinction that remains one of the most practically useful in all of decision theory: the difference between **risk** and **uncertainty**.

Risk describes situations in which the outcomes are unknown but the probability distribution over those outcomes is known or can be reliably estimated. Rolling a fair die: the outcome is uncertain, but the probability of each face is exactly 1/6. An insurance actuary calculating mortality risk for a large population: the individual deaths are unpredictable, but the aggregate rate is estimable with high confidence from historical data. In risky situations, the Expected Value framework applies directly.

Uncertainty (what Knight called "true uncertainty" or Knightian uncertainty) describes situations in which the probability distribution itself is unknown or unknowable. The outcome of a genuinely novel technological development, the trajectory of a relationship through an unprecedented life transition, the consequence of a policy applied to a complex adaptive system for the first time. In uncertain situations, there is no stable probability to plug into the EV formula. The formula's application is speculative rather than calculable.

The practical implication is not that uncertain situations should be avoided—many of the most consequential decisions in life involve genuine uncertainty. It is that the correct cognitive mode for uncertain situations is different from the correct mode for risky ones. In risky situations, calculate expected values and optimize. In uncertain situations, emphasize **robustness**: choose actions that produce acceptable outcomes across a wide range of possible futures, rather than actions that are optimal in the expected case but catastrophic in the tails. Maintain optionality. Avoid irreversible commitments until the distribution becomes clearer.

5.8 The Probability Disciplines: Three Applied Practices

The Pre-Mortem

Before committing to a significant decision, conduct a structured imagining of its failure. Project yourself twelve months into a future in which the decision produced the worst plausible outcome. Working from that vantage point, generate the most credible account of how the failure occurred. What sequence of events, what overlooked risks, what incorrect assumptions, what external shocks produced this outcome?

The pre-mortem, developed by psychologist Gary Klein, is the most effective known technique for surfacing failure modes that optimism suppresses during forward-looking analysis. It exploits the brain's facility for narrative construction and applies it in service of risk identification rather than fantasy. The failure modes it surfaces can then be incorporated into the probability estimate and, where possible, addressed in the decision design.

The Outside View

For any significant forward-looking estimate—a project timeline, a revenue forecast, a probability of success for a new endeavor—systematically consult the base rate before constructing the inside view. Find the reference class of comparable situations and ask: what fraction of projects like this, at this stage, succeeded? What was the median timeline? What fraction ran significantly over?

The outside view almost always produces more accurate estimates than the inside view—the detailed analysis of the specific situation that feels more rigorous but is more vulnerable to optimism bias and narrative construction. Use the outside view to anchor the estimate, then adjust for features that genuinely distinguish your situation from the reference class. Resist the very strong temptation to conclude that your situation is so distinctive that the base rate does not apply.

The Decision Journal

Keep a brief record of significant decisions: the date, the decision, the key reasoning, the estimated probabilities of key outcomes, and a scheduled review date. When the review date arrives, return to the entry and compare actual outcomes to estimated probabilities. Over time, this record reveals your systematic biases—whether you are consistently overoptimistic about timelines, whether your risk estimates are well-calibrated, whether you are responsive to contrary evidence.

The decision journal is the personal equivalent of the scoring system used in forecasting tournaments. It makes the invisible visible—converting the diffuse sense that your decision-making is "pretty good" into a trackable record that either confirms that assessment or provides specific, actionable information about where it needs to improve.

5.9 Prospect Theory: The Shape of How We Feel About Outcomes

Kahneman and Tversky's most enduring contribution to decision science was not the catalogue of biases but the mathematical model they built to describe how people actually evaluate outcomes under uncertainty. **Prospect Theory**, published in 1979, replaced the classical Expected Utility model with a framework that accurately predicts the full range of human decision-making errors—not just identifying them but explaining the specific shape of the distortions.

Prospect Theory has two key components.

The first is a **value function** with three properties: it is defined over gains and losses relative to a reference point (not absolute wealth), it is concave in the gain domain (we are risk-averse when facing potential gains), and it is convex in the loss domain (we are risk-seeking when facing potential losses). Most importantly, the loss curve is steeper than the gain curve—the mathematical formalization of loss aversion.

$$
v(x) = \begin{cases} x^\alpha & x \geq 0 \\ -\lambda(-x)^\beta & x < 0 \end{cases}
\tag{5.4}
$$

Where $\lambda > 1$ is the loss aversion coefficient (typically estimated at approximately 2–2.5 in experimental settings) and $\alpha, \beta \in (0, 1)$ capture the diminishing sensitivity to larger magnitudes of gain and loss.

The second component is a **probability weighting function**: the transformation of objective probabilities into decision weights, which are not the same thing. People systematically overweight small probabilities (which explains the appeal of both lottery tickets and insurance for catastrophic-but-unlikely events) and underweight moderate-to-large probabilities (which explains risk aversion in the moderate-probability, moderate-gain domain where most real decisions live).

The practical implication of both components is that emotional decision-making is not merely inaccurate—it is systematically and predictably inaccurate in specific directions. The shape of the distortions tells you exactly where the corrections need to be applied:

- When a decision involves a small-probability catastrophic loss: your emotional response is likely over-weighting the probability. Calculate it. The number is almost always smaller than your emotional response implies.

- When a decision involves moderate-probability gains: your emotional response is likely underweighting the probability and over-discounting the expected value. The bet is almost always more favorable than it feels.

- When a decision involves potential losses from your current position: loss aversion is inflating the cost. Reframe by asking what the correct EV calculation implies, rather than how the loss would feel.

5.10 Probabilistic Thinking as a Daily Practice

The biases catalogued in this chapter do not disappear once you have read about them. Knowing about loss aversion does not prevent you from experiencing the full emotional force of potential loss. The corrective is not insight but **procedure**—a set of habituated practices that engage the analytical system before the emotional response has already committed to a direction.

Practice 1: The probability question. Before any significant decision that involves uncertainty, write down your explicit probability estimates for the key outcomes. Not vague hedges ("I think it will probably work") but numbers: $P_{\text{win}} = 0.65$, $P_{\text{loss}} = 0.35$. The act of writing a number forces confrontation with the uncertainty in a way that verbal hedging does not.

Practice 2: The reference class anchor. For any forward-looking estimate, identify the base rate before constructing the inside view. What fraction of comparable situations ended in the outcome you are estimating? Anchor to that number and then adjust for the specific features that genuinely distinguish your situation from the reference class. Resist the very human impulse to conclude immediately that your situation is so distinctive that the base rate does not apply.

Practice 3: The adversarial check. Before finalizing any significant judgment, spend five minutes generating the strongest possible case for the opposite conclusion. Not to change your mind, but to ensure that your probability estimate is robust to the opposing argument. If the opposing case dissolves immediately, your confidence is well-founded. If it is difficult to dismiss, your probability estimate should reflect that difficulty.

Practice 4: The sunk cost interrupt. When you notice yourself reluctant to abandon a course of action primarily because of how much has already been invested in it, ask explicitly: *"If I had not already invested anything in this, and someone offered me the opportunity to begin from exactly this* *point, would I take it?"* If yes, continue. If no, the sunk cost is distorting the forward-looking calculus, and the rational action is to stop.

Practice 5: The 10-10-10 frame. For decisions with significant emotional charge, evaluate the choice across three time horizons: How will I feel about this in ten minutes? In ten months? In ten years? This simple reframing shifts attention from the emotionally dominant near-term to the full temporal scope of the decision's consequences, often revealing that the emotional urgency of the immediate moment is poorly calibrated to the long-run significance of the choice.

> *Quality of Decisions = EV Calculation + Calibrated Probabilities + Bias Correction*

5.11 Risk Tolerance vs. Risk Capacity: An Important Distinction

A final distinction that probabilistic thinking demands but popular discourse conflates is the difference between **risk tolerance** and **risk capacity**.

Risk tolerance is a psychological property: the level of uncertainty and potential loss that a person can emotionally sustain without making destructive decisions. Someone with high risk tolerance can watch a portfolio drop 40% without panic selling; someone with low risk tolerance cannot.

Risk capacity is a structural property: the level of uncertainty and potential loss that a person's actual financial, professional, and temporal situation can absorb without catastrophic consequence. Someone with six months of emergency savings and no dependents has high risk capacity; someone with no savings, high fixed expenses, and dependents has low risk capacity regardless of their emotional risk tolerance.

The rational risk level is determined by the *minimum* of these two: a person with high risk tolerance but low risk capacity should not take high risks, because the structural consequences of loss would be catastrophic regardless of how emotionally manageable the experience feels. A person with high risk capacity but low risk tolerance should not take low risks indefinitely, because they are leaving expected value on the table due to emotional calibration alone—and that emotional calibration can be improved through gradual exposure and education in a way that structural risk capacity cannot always be.

Most people conflate the two and evaluate their risk level based on their emotional tolerance alone, without analyzing whether their structural situation can support that tolerance. The mathematical thinker assesses both, applies the minimum, and works deliberately to expand both over time.

Chapter Logic Check

☐ In my most important pending decision, have I calculated a genuine *EV*—with explicit probability estimates, not vague optimism—or am I relying on the feeling that it will probably work out?

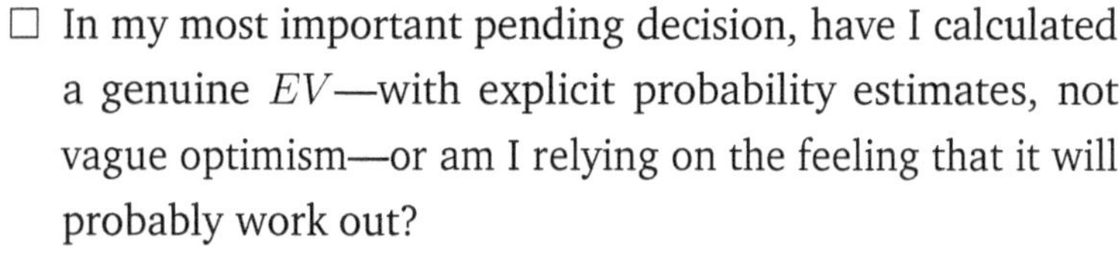

☐ What is the reference class for this decision, and what is the base-rate probability of success for that class? Have I anchored to that number before adjusting?

☐ What is the single most important piece of new evidence I
have received in the past month that I have not yet updated
my beliefs in response to?

Chapter 6

The Law of Compounding: The Exponential Secret

"Compound interest is the eighth wonder of the world. He who understands it, earns it; he who doesn't, pays it."
—attributed to Albert Einstein

6.1 The Penny That Broke Intuition

Here is a question that has been asked and answered millions of times, and that continues to produce the wrong answer from the vast majority of people who hear it for the first time.

You are offered a choice. Option A: receive one million dollars today, as a lump sum, tax-free, immediately. Option B: receive a single penny today, which will double in value every day for thirty days.

Most people, when confronted with this question quickly, choose Option A without serious deliberation. One million dollars is a concrete, definable, life-altering sum. A penny is a penny. The comparison seems asymmetric to the point of absurdity.

The mathematics is equally asymmetric—in the opposite direction.

$$V_t = 0.01 \times 2^{t-1} \qquad (6.1)$$

On Day 10, the penny is worth \$5.12. On Day 15, it is worth \$163.84. On Day 20, it is worth \$5,242.88—still less than one percent of Option A's value, and still apparently confirming the choice of Option A as obviously correct. On Day 25, it is worth \$167,772.16. On Day 29, it is worth \$2,684,354.56. On Day 30, it is worth \$5,368,709.12.

Five and a half million dollars. Five times the value of Option A. From a penny.

The magnitude of the error in the initial intuition is not the interesting part. The interesting part is where the error was made. The person who chooses Option A is not failing at arithmetic. They are failing at visualization—at the ability to construct a mental model of what exponential growth looks like across time. This failure is nearly universal because the human visual cortex and the intuitive number sense that evolved with it are both calibrated for linear patterns. We can easily imagine the difference between ten and twenty, or between one hundred and two hundred. We cannot easily imagine the difference between 2^{20} and 2^{30}.

The result is a systematic, lifelong undervaluation of processes that compound.

6.2 Linear Thinking in an Exponential World

The gap between linear and exponential thinking is not merely an abstract mathematical curiosity. It is the operating error that explains a substantial fraction of the frustration people experience with long-term development processes of every kind.

Linear growth adds a constant amount per period: $1, 2, 3, 4, 5 \ldots$ The graph is a straight line. Progress is uniform, visible, and psychologically satisfying because each period delivers approximately the same increment as the last.

Exponential growth multiplies by a constant factor per period: $1, 2, 4, 8, 16 \ldots$ The graph is a curve that appears nearly flat at the beginning and then rises steeply—with the vast majority of total growth occurring in the final periods. Progress is not uniform. It is invisible for a long time and then dramatic all at once.

The practical problem is that most meaningful development processes are exponential in structure but evaluated by people using linear intuitions. A person learning a new language expects their conversational fluency to grow by roughly equal increments each month. In reality, the early months build foundational infrastructure that is invisible in conversations—phonological patterns, grammatical rules, core vocabulary networks—and the fluency stock grows slowly while this infrastructure is being laid. Then, past some threshold of foundation, the stock compounds rapidly: each new word learned activates connections to dozens of words already acquired, and each conversation builds on the entire accumulated base.

The same structure governs fitness (slow early adaptation of neurological recruitment patterns before visible strength gains); skill acquisition in cognitive domains (slow early pattern-learning before visible performance improvements); business development (slow early network-building before visible revenue acceleration); and investment returns (slow early accumulation before the compounding begins to move large absolute numbers).

Every one of these processes has a characteristic shape: long flat base, sharp rise late. And every one of them produces the same experience in the early phases: the suspicion, increasingly difficult to resist, that the process is not working.

6.3 The Anatomy of the Compound Curve

The general formula for compound growth is:

$$A = P \left(1 + \frac{r}{n}\right)^{nt} \tag{6.2}$$

Where:

- A: The final accumulated value.

- P: The principal—the starting value of the stock being compounded (savings, skill, reputation, fitness).

- r: The periodic improvement rate—the fraction by which the stock grows per compounding period.

- n: The number of compounding periods per unit of time.

- t: The total elapsed time.

The most important structural observation about this formula is the location of t: it is in the exponent. This means that time does not *add to* the accumulated value; it *multiplies* everything that has accumulated before it. Each additional period of compounding does not contribute a constant amount but a constant fraction of an ever-larger base. This is why the compound curve appears flat at the beginning and steep at the end—the absolute increment per period is growing proportionally to the base, which is itself growing.

A concrete comparison makes this vivid. Consider two individuals, both saving at 10% annual returns, but with different starting ages.

- **Person A** invests $5,000 per year from age 22 to age 32 (10 years), then stops entirely and allows the accumulated amount to grow untouched until age 62.

- **Person B** invests $5,000 per year from age 32 to age 62 (30 years)—three times as long as Person A.

At age 62, Person A has accumulated approximately $1,078,000. Person B, who invested three times as many years and three times as much total capital, has accumulated approximately $904,000. Person A ends with more money despite investing for a fraction of the time and a fraction of the total dollars—not because of any advantage in rate or skill, but because of the location of their contributions in the timeline of the compounding process. The early investment captured the long tail of the exponent. The late investment, however intensive, missed it.

This is not a financial curiosity. It is a mathematical demonstration of the most counterintuitive property of compound growth: **the value of early action is disproportionate to the effort of early action.** Starting earlier—in investment, in skill development, in relationship building, in any compounding domain—produces advantages that later effort cannot fully compensate.

6.4 The Valley of Disappointment

The compound curve's characteristic shape creates a phase of development that is so consistently discouraging, and so consistently misinterpreted, that it deserves a specific name. The **Valley of Disappointment** is the early period of a compounding process during which the growth rate, measured in absolute terms, is nearly invisible—and during which the distance between expected progress (based on linear intuition) and actual progress (based on exponential reality) is at its widest.

$$Success = Consistency \times Time^{Effort}$$

The Valley of Disappointment is the period in which most people quit. Not because the process has failed. Not because the rate of growth is insufficient. But because the *absolute increment* in any given period is small, and the brain, calibrated for linear evaluation, interprets small absolute increments as evidence of a broken process rather than as evidence of a process doing exactly what a compounding process does in its early phase.

The writer who has been publishing for six months and has not yet built a meaningful audience is not failing—they are accumulating foundational readership infrastructure. The fitness practitioner whose body composition has not visibly changed after twelve weeks of training is not failing—they are building neurological and metabolic adaptations that precede visible changes. The entrepreneur whose business is generating modest revenue after a year of sustained effort is not failing—they are compounding the customer relationships, operational knowledge, and market reputation that constitute the base of the exponential rise.

The Valley does not last forever. But it lasts long enough—characteristically between six months and three years depending on the domain—that it requires a deliberate intellectual commitment to survive it intact. That commitment is not willpower. It is **mathematical literacy**: the understanding that the flat phase is not a failure signal but a loading phase. The curve is not broken. The exponent is building.

6.5 The Reliability Constant: Why Zeros Are Fatal

The compound growth formula contains a property that most discussions of compounding overlook entirely, and that is in some respects more important than the growth rate itself. It is what might be called the **Reliability Constant**—the requirement that the compounding process continue without interruption.

Consider a simplified version: a process that multiplies a stock by a constant factor k each period, producing $P \times k^t$ after t periods. The accumulated value after ten periods at $k = 1.01$ (1% growth per period) is:

$$P \times 1.01^{10} = P \times 1.105 \tag{6.3}$$

A 10.5% total gain. Modest but real. Now consider what happens if a single period in the chain produces not growth but a zero—a period in which the activity is abandoned, the habit is broken, the contribution is skipped:

$$P \times 1.01^4 \times 0 \times 1.01^5 = P \times 1.041 \times 0 \times 1.051 = 0$$

The accumulated value is zero. Every period of growth before the zero is erased. Every period after it begins from zero rather than from the accumulated base. The zero does not merely subtract from the total; it multiplies the total by zero and destroys the exponent.

This property of multiplication is well known in arithmetic. Its implications for habit formation, consistent practice, and long-term development are less widely internalized.

Consistency is not merely a virtue in a compounding system. It is the structural requirement. A process that produces 50% growth per period but is interrupted every fifth period is not a better compounding engine than one that produces 1% growth per period with perfect continuity. The interrupted process never builds the exponential base from which the steep rise emerges. The consistent process does.

This is the mathematical argument for systems that prioritize sustainability over intensity. The aggressive training program that produces visible results quickly but carries a high injury rate is, from a compounding perspective, worse than the modest program that produces unremarkable results in any single week but never introduces a zero into the sequence. The injury, the illness, the burnout, the abandonment—each of these is a zero, and each zero resets the exponent.

Building the Reliability Constant means designing your compounding systems to be **foolproof at minimum viable level**, not merely optimal at maximum motivation level. The question is not "what would I do if everything went right?" but "what is the smallest execution of this process that I can sustain even when things go wrong?" That minimum viable version—executed every day without exception—produces

more compounding value over ten years than the optimal
version executed on the good days.

6.6 The Rate Variable: Small Differences, Large Consequences

The growth rate r in the compound formula is easy to under-value in the short run because its effects are invisible until the exponent has had time to amplify them. But over the long periods that matter for significant life outcomes, small differences in rate produce enormous differences in accumulated value.

Consider the difference between daily improvement rates of 1% and 0.5%:

$$\text{At 1\% per day for 365 days:} \quad 1.01^{365} \approx 37.8 \qquad (6.4)$$

$$\text{At 0.5\% per day for 365 days:} \quad 1.005^{365} \approx 6.2 \qquad (6.5)$$

A twofold difference in daily rate produces a sixfold difference in annual outcome. The first produces a return of 3,678%; the second produces a return of 520%. The daily difference—a fraction of a percentage point—is not perceptible in any given day. Across a year, it is the difference between a transformative outcome and a modest one.

The compounding of rate differences compounds itself. The person with a slightly higher daily learning rate does not merely learn a little more each day; they build a larger knowledge base from which subsequent learning draws, which increases the effective learning rate further. The person who reads ten pages daily does not merely accumulate more pages than the person who reads five; they develop stronger comprehension, broader associative networks, and faster pattern recognition, all of which accelerate the rate of knowledge acquisition in subsequent reading.

This dynamic—where a small rate advantage compounds into an accelerating structural advantage—is the mathematical basis of what Malcolm Gladwell popularized as the "10,000-hour rule" and what researchers in skill acquisition call the **power law of practice**. Early marginal advantages in practice quality or frequency compound, through the structure of skill-building itself, into later large advantages in performance.

$$A = P(1 + r/n)^{nt} \text{ — } Small\ r,\ Large\ t,\ Never\ Zero$$

6.7 Negative Compounding: The Mirror Image

Every principle of compounding operates in reverse with equal mathematical force.

Debt at 20% annual interest compounds exactly as savings at 20% annual returns would—but in the direction of the creditor's benefit rather than yours. Bad habits do not merely produce bad outcomes in the periods they are practiced; they degrade the physical, cognitive, and social capital that future outcomes compound upon. Neglected relationships do not merely lose value in periods of neglect; they lose the trust stock that makes future positive interactions more valuable.

The insight that compounding operates symmetrically—that it works for you when positive rates are maintained consistently, and against you when negative rates are maintained consistently—is both sobering and instructive. Many of the chronic difficulties people experience in their financial, physical, and relational lives are not the result of discrete bad decisions but of modest negative compounding rates maintained over long periods. The credit card balance that has been carried for seven years. The fitness decline that has accumulated at -0.5% per week. The friendship that has received one fewer meaningful interaction per month for three years.

In each case, the absolute magnitude of the problem in any single period is small. The cumulative magnitude, compounded over the elapsed time, is large. And because negative compounding is as invisible in its early phases as positive compounding, the problem frequently becomes visible only when it has already reached a level that requires substantial corrective effort to reverse.

The corrective frame: identify the stocks in your life that are currently experiencing negative net flows and calculate what the compounding trajectory implies at the current rate over five and ten years. The result of this calculation is, in most cases, highly motivating. Modest, sustainable improvements in flow rates—the kind that feel too small to matter in a single week—produce dramatically different ten-year trajectories when compounding is correctly accounted for.

6.8 Compounding Across Domains

Financial Compounding

The financial application is the one most commonly associated with the compound growth formula, and it is where the mathematics is most precisely quantifiable. The essential principles: start early (the exponent is your ally, and time cannot be recovered); maintain consistency (the zero that resets the exponent is often an emergency that a buffer fund would have absorbed); minimize the friction costs that reduce the effective rate (fees, taxes, and high-cost debt are negative flows that compound against you).

The single most powerful financial decision most people can make is not which investments to choose but when to start. A 25-year-old who invests modestly and consistently is, from a compounding standpoint, in a fundamentally different position than a 40-year-old who invests aggressively. The early investor has the exponent on their side. The late investor is competing against it.

Skill Compounding

Skills compound through what researchers call the **knowledge spiral**: existing knowledge makes new knowledge easier to acquire, because new information has more existing structures to connect to, more prior patterns to activate, and more contextual meaning available. An expert learns faster in their domain than a novice not only because they have better judgment about what to study but because the physical structure of their knowledge network facilitates faster encoding of new material.

The implication: invest in foundational skills early and deeply, because the foundations are the principal upon which all subsequent skill-building compounds. Breadth that has no foundation compounds poorly; depth in a foundational domain creates the network structure from which related domains can be learned rapidly.

Relational Compounding

Trust compounds. A relationship that has accumulated a large stock of trust—through years of reliable, reciprocal, honest interactions—can absorb a negative event that would destroy a newer relationship, because the trust principal buffers the loss. Conversely, a relationship that has accumulated a deficit of trust—through small consistent failures of reliability or reciprocity—becomes progressively less capable of repair as the deficit compounds.

The relational compounding insight is that the value of a consistent small positive interaction far exceeds its face-value impression. Each instance of following through on a small commitment, each unsolicited acknowledgment, each moment of genuine attention, is not merely a pleasant interaction; it is a flow into the trust stock, building the compounding principal that makes the relationship progressively more valuable and more resilient.

6.9 Engineering Your Compounding System

The practical architecture for leveraging compounding in any domain has three components.

Identify the principal: What is the stock you are trying to build? Be specific enough to measure. Not "my career" but "my demonstrable competency in data visualization, as measured by the complexity of projects I can execute independently."

Protect the exponent: Design the minimum viable version of the daily or weekly practice—the version you can sustain without exception, including during illness, travel, high-stress periods, and motivational troughs. This is the Reliability Constant in practice. It is not the optimal version; it is the unbreakable floor.

Optimize the rate within sustainability: Within the constraint of the Reliability Constant, maximize the quality and specificity of the practice. Focused, targeted effort produces higher r than diffuse effort at equal time investment. Deliberate practice—practice organized around specific gaps and feedback—compounds faster than undirected repetition.

The compound curve will not lie to you. If the three components are in place—a defined principal, a protected exponent, and an optimized rate—the curve will do exactly what the mathematics says it will do. It will appear to produce nothing for a long time. And then it will produce everything.

6.10 The Rule of 72: Compounding as a Mental Shortcut

The full compound growth formula is precise but computationally demanding for mental arithmetic. The **Rule of 72** provides a practical shortcut that makes compounding instantly legible in everyday situations.

Dividing 72 by the annual growth rate (expressed as a percentage) gives the approximate number of years required to double the accumulated value:

$$T_{\text{double}} \approx \frac{72}{r \times 100} \tag{6.6}$$

At 6% annual growth, the stock doubles in approximately 12 years. At 9%, it doubles in 8 years. At 12%, in 6 years. At 1%—the rate of many savings accounts until recently—it takes

72 years to double. The Rule of 72 converts an abstract growth rate into an intuitive time horizon, making the consequences of rate differences immediately visceral.

The same rule applies to negative compounding. A habit that degrades a stock at 6% per year halves the stock in 12 years. A credit card with a 24% annual interest rate doubles the debt in 3 years. A savings account in an inflation environment of 4% halves its purchasing power in 18 years. Negative compounding operates with the same mathematics as positive compounding; the Rule of 72 makes both directions equally legible.

The most practically important application of the Rule of 72 is in evaluating investment and debt decisions in real time, without a spreadsheet. Should you accept a deal that offers a 4% annual return when your outstanding credit card debt charges 20%? The Rule tells you: the debt is doubling in 3.6 years; the investment doubles in 18. The answer is no, by a very large margin. This reasoning, available in seconds, is more immediately useful than any spreadsheet output for the everyday financial decisions that have the largest compounding consequences.

6.11 Compounding Identity and Self-Concept

The compounding principle applies not only to measurable stocks—savings, skills, fitness—but to the most consequential stock of all: **identity**. What a person believes to be true about themselves functions as a constraint on the compound curve of their development. An identity that centers on limitation— "I am not good with money," "I am not a technical person," "I am not the kind of person who exercises consistently"—sets the effective growth rate of the corresponding stock to zero or negative. The identity functions as a zero in the multiplication chain.

Conversely, an identity organized around process rather than fixed traits—"I am someone who consistently takes one step forward in my financial situation each month," "I am someone who develops new skills deliberately"—treats the identity itself as a compounding stock. Each small action consistent with this process-identity strengthens it; the identity and the behavior reinforce each other in a positively reinforcing loop.

The behavioral psychology research on this phenomenon is extensive and consistent: behavior change is more durable when it is connected to identity change than when it is maintained by willpower or external motivation alone. The mechanism is precisely the compound feedback loop: acting consistently with an identity reinforces the identity, which makes subsequent consistent action feel more natural, which reinforces the identity further.

$$Identity(t) = Actions\ Taken + Narrative\ About\ Those\ Actions \times Time$$

This has a practical prescription: when building a new compounding system, articulate explicitly the identity that the system serves. Not "I am trying to exercise more" but "I am someone who treats physical maintenance as a non-negotiable daily practice." The identity statement is not a self-deception; it is a deliberate choice of the reference standard against which behavior is measured. Behavior tends to regress toward the identity baseline. Set the baseline correctly, and the regression is a correction toward the desired behavior rather than away from it.

The compounding of identity also explains a frequently underappreciated feature of major life change: why it is so difficult to sustain. When behavior changes faster than identity, the new behavior lacks the reinforcing support of an identity-consistent narrative. It feels effortful, foreign, and fragile—because it is all three. Durable behavior change requires that the identity stock eventually catch up to the behavioral change, at which point the behavior feels not like discipline but like expression of self. This catch-up takes time—typically months rather than days—and occurs through the same compound mechanism as every other stock: consistent small flows in the right direction, maintained without interruption until the new base is established.

Chapter Logic Check

☐ In the domain most important to me right now, am I currently in the Valley of Disappointment—and if so, can I calculate what the exponent implies about my position at the same rate in three years?

☐ What is the minimum viable version of my most important daily practice—the floor below which I will not fall even on the worst days, ensuring I never introduce a zero into the sequence?

☐ Where in my life is a modest negative compounding rate currently accumulating—a debt, a neglected relationship, a declining health metric—and what is the projected ten-year outcome at the current rate?

Chapter 7

Removing Cognitive Noise: The Signal-to-Noise Ratio

> *"It is not the strongest of the species that survives, nor the most intelligent. It is the one most responsive to change."*
>
> —often attributed to Charles Darwin

7.1 The Bandwidth Crisis

In 1948, Claude Shannon published a paper that created the field of information theory. One of its central findings was a mathematical relationship between the capacity of a communication channel, the bandwidth of the signal, and the power of background noise. Shannon's theorem established that the maximum rate at which information can be reliably transmitted through a noisy channel is fundamentally bounded—not by the power of the transmitter, but by the ratio of signal power to noise power.

You can increase the transmitter's power indefinitely, but if the noise increases at the same rate, the information capacity does not improve. The only reliable path to better information transmission is reducing the noise.

Shannon was describing radio channels. He was also, as it turns out, describing the human mind in the twenty-first century.

The average adult in a connected society is exposed to an estimated 34 gigabytes of information per day—a figure that has grown by roughly 5% annually since the early 1980s. This is not information that was sought out; it is information that arrives automatically, through the same attention-capture systems that delivered it to the previous attention-holder and will deliver it to the next. The pipeline runs continuously and does not discriminate by relevance or quality. It delivers viral misinformation and landmark research with equal urgency. It presents the anxiety-inducing headline and the trivial brand promotion with equal prominence. It cannot, by design, tell the difference between what matters to you and what is merely loud.

The result is a cognitive bandwidth crisis. Not a shortage of information—information has never been more abundant—but a shortage of the mental clarity required to extract what is genuinely useful from an environment optimized to overwhelm rather than illuminate.

The mathematical framework for addressing this crisis comes from the same source as its diagnosis. Shannon's insight applies in both directions: if the path to better information transmission is reducing noise, then the path to clearer thinking is not consuming more high-quality information. It is eliminating more low-quality noise. The leverage is in the denominator.

7.2 The Signal-to-Noise Ratio

The **Signal-to-Noise Ratio** (SNR) measures the relative power of useful information to background interference:

$$SNR = \frac{P_{\text{signal}}}{P_{\text{noise}}} \qquad (7.1)$$

A high SNR means the useful information is easily distinguishable from the noise. A low SNR means the signal is buried, distorted, and difficult to interpret accurately. Shannon established that below a certain SNR threshold, reliable information transmission becomes impossible regardless of how the receiver processes the signal—the noise is simply too dense to see through.

In practical cognitive terms:

- **Signal** is information that directly informs a decision you will actually make, develops a skill or understanding with measurable value, or connects to a goal currently in your priority stack. Signal is high-leverage, purposeful, and in service of something specific.

- **Noise** is information that generates cognitive activity without producing actionable output: social media outrage, speculative commentary on events you cannot influence, trivial updates, opinion content that reinforces beliefs you already hold without deepening them, and the chronic low-grade urgency of notifications designed to capture attention rather than deliver value.

The distinction is not about the subject matter of the information. Noise is not synonymous with entertainment or leisure, and Signal is not synonymous with work or productivity. A novel that develops empathy and narrative understanding is Signal. A social media scroll that consumes forty minutes and produces no memory of its content is Noise. A difficult conversation that clears a genuine misunderstanding is Signal. A podcast that provides the sensation of learning without producing any lasting change in understanding or behavior is Noise.

The critical test: **Does engaging with this information change how I will think or act?** If yes, Signal. If no—if the interaction leaves your decisions, beliefs, and behaviors exactly where they were—Noise.

7.3 The Noise Amplification Mechanism

Modern information systems are not designed to optimize your SNR. They are designed to maximize engagement—the total time and attention devoted to the platform—which is a very different objective. Engagement is maximized by content that produces strong emotional arousal: outrage, anxiety, tribalism, and social comparison. These emotional states are evolutionarily ancient and extremely attention-capturing. They are also, in almost all cases, antithetical to clear, strategic, long-horizon thinking.

The mechanism is straightforward. Attention-capture systems use behavioral feedback loops to identify, for each user, the content most likely to produce the next interaction—the next click, the next scroll, the next share. Content that produces outrage generates more interactions than content that produces calm reflection, because outrage is a higher-arousal state. Over time, the feedback loop selects for progressively more extreme, emotionally activating content—not because the designers are malicious, but because the optimization target (engagement) is structurally misaligned with the user's interest (clear, calm, accurate thinking).

The result is that the average information consumer, navigating the modern environment without deliberate filtering, is not being exposed to the world's most important and accurate information. They are being exposed to the world's most emotionally activating information. These are not the same thing. In many domains, they are nearly opposite.

The mathematical implication: **the default information environment systematically lowers your** SNR. It is an environment calibrated to maximize noise consumption. Operating effectively within it requires active countermeasures—not passive consumption with good intentions.

$$Cognitive\ Clarity = \frac{Signal\ Consumed}{Total\ Information\ Consumed}$$

7.4 First-Order and Second-Order Thinking

One of noise's most effective disguises is the first-order solution—an action, decision, or piece of information that appears to address a problem but actually addresses only its most immediate manifestation while generating a larger second-order problem downstream.

$$Outcome = E_1 \rightarrow E_2 \rightarrow E_3 \rightarrow \ldots$$

First-order thinking evaluates E_1—the immediate consequence of an action. It is fast, emotionally satisfying, and almost always incorrect as a model of complex situations because complex situations almost never terminate at E_1. Every action produces a consequence that itself becomes a cause of the next consequence, which becomes a cause of the next, in a chain that extends well beyond the time horizon of emotional decision-making.

Second-order thinking evaluates the full sequence—E_1, then E_2, then E_3—and weighs each against its probability and time horizon. It is slower, requires deliberate effort, and is often emotionally unsatisfying because the correct second-order action frequently involves accepting a first-order cost in exchange for a second-order benefit.

Examples of noise disguised as first-order solutions:

Consuming more information in response to anxiety. The first-order effect is the reduction of uncertainty—each new piece of information temporarily fills the gap that was producing the anxious feeling. The second-order effect is an increase in the total volume of conflicting, low-quality information in the cognitive system, which increases uncertainty over the medium term. The correct second-order intervention is often the opposite: reduce information input and work with the information already held.

Avoiding difficult conversations. The first-order effect is the relief of not having the conversation. The second-order effect is the accumulation of unresolved tension that makes the eventual conversation more difficult and the relationship more fragile. The difficulty deferred is difficulty compounded.

Over-scheduling in response to the feeling of being behind. The first-order effect is the psychological comfort of a full calendar—evidence of productivity, of effort, of commitment. The second-order effect is the elimination of the unstructured thinking time that generates the insights and decisions that would actually resolve the backlog. Busyness, paradoxically, compounds the problem it was recruited to solve.

7.5 Information Entropy and the Lindy Effect

In thermodynamics, **entropy** is the measure of disorder in a system. Without active energy input, closed systems drift toward maximum entropy—the state of uniform randomness in which no structure or gradient exists. The second law of thermodynamics holds that this drift is the default direction of all physical systems absent deliberate intervention.

The cognitive analogue is exact. Without active filtering— a deliberate, maintained effort to curate the information environment—the mind exposed to the modern information ecosystem drifts toward maximum cognitive entropy: an un-differentiated flood of inputs with no hierarchy of reliability, no structure of relevance, and no framework for distinguish-ing the consequential from the trivial. The drift is not a failure of character. It is the default behavior of any system without an active entropy-reduction process.

The most reliable heuristic for information entropy reduc-tion is the **Lindy Effect**, named after the Lindy's deli in New York where the concept was informally discussed by intellec-tuals in the 1960s and later formalized by Nassim Nicholas Taleb. The Lindy Effect holds that the future life expectancy of a non-perishable item—an idea, a technology, an institution, a practice—is proportional to its current age. A book that has been in continuous print for one hundred years has already survived one hundred years of competition with alternatives and critique from a changing world. Its survival is evidence of something—durability, depth, genuine utility—that a book published last month has not yet demonstrated.

This is not a conservative or nostalgic argument. It is a probabilistic one. Novel information has not been stress-tested. It has not passed through the filter of time, which is the only filter that reliably removes the false from the durable. Consuming primarily novel information means consuming primarily untested claims—with a signal embedded in substantial noise. Consuming primarily Lindy-tested information means consuming material that has already been filtered, at lower noise cost.

The practical application: weight your information consumption toward sources that have demonstrated durability. Books that have been read for decades. Frameworks that have been applied across generations. Primary sources rather than commentary. Data that has been replicated rather than findings that have been reported once. The goal is not to ignore the new but to calibrate the trust assigned to it relative to its track record.

7.6 Attention as a Finite Resource

In the economic theory of attention, developed by Herbert Simon and extended by many subsequent researchers, **attention** is the limiting resource of the information age—the constraint that, in Shannon's terms, determines the maximum rate at which information can be usefully processed. Information is abundant and becoming more so. Attention is fixed. The scarcity has shifted.

This has a direct implication for the value of your attention as an asset: it is more valuable than the information that competes to consume it. Every piece of information you choose to engage with is purchasing some fraction of your attention at a price—the opportunity cost of what else that attention could have produced.

The attention economy—the system of advertising, social media, and content distribution that funds most of the internet—does not pay you for your attention. It sells it. You are not the customer; you are the inventory. The platforms' business model is to acquire your attention at zero direct cost to you (by providing free services) and resell it to advertisers at a profit. The transaction is invisible and voluntary, but its economics are precise: your attention has a market price, and you are consistently receiving zero of it.

Understanding attention as a finite, valuable asset—one whose allocation determines the quality of your thinking and decision-making—converts the question of information consumption from a lifestyle choice into a resource management problem. The same Variable Audit from Chapter One applies: what information inputs are generating genuine signal, what are generating noise, and what is the net effect on the quality of the decisions that the information is ostensibly informing?

7.7 The Noise Reduction Protocol

The following is a practical protocol for systematically improving your cognitive SNR. It is not a one-time exercise but a periodic maintenance process, applied on the same rhythm as the review gates in Chapter Two.

Step 1: Inventory your inputs. List every regular information source you consume: news, social media platforms, podcasts, email subscriptions, messaging channels, colleagues, and informal social inputs. For each, estimate the average weekly time investment.

Step 2: Apply the Signal test. For each source, ask: In the past month, did something I consumed from this source change how I thought about something important, informed a decision I actually made, or developed a capacity I actually used? If yes—and if you can name the specific instance—it is at least partially Signal. If no, it is likely primarily Noise.

Step 3: Calculate the SNR for each source. What fraction of the content consumed from this source passes the Signal test? A source where 5% of content is Signal has an SNR of roughly 0.05. A source where 60% is Signal has an SNR of roughly 0.6.

Step 4: Sort by SNR and apply the cutoff. Rank your sources by SNR. Eliminate or dramatically reduce consumption from sources below a threshold you define. The threshold should be set at a level that feels uncomfortable—a level that requires actually removing sources rather than merely intending to.

Step 5: Protect the recovered attention. The attention recovered by noise reduction is only valuable if it is directed somewhere. Identify the Signal sources that are currently under-consumed due to attention scarcity—the books unfinished, the deep work unstarted, the conversations unmade—and explicitly allocate the recovered capacity there.

7.8 Cognitive Noise in Three Domains

Professional Noise

In knowledge work, the most common forms of cognitive noise are reactive communication (responding to messages as they arrive rather than in scheduled windows), meeting attendance without a defined decision or output, and status-tracking—the monitoring of metrics, dashboards, and social media responses that generates the sensation of productivity without producing it.

The Signal test applied to professional behavior: Does this activity directly advance a defined deliverable, inform a pending decision, or develop a skill I have prioritized? If not, it is professional noise—and it carries the same opportunity cost as any other noise, measured in attention displaced from the work that actually matters.

Financial Noise

In personal finance, the most destructive noise is short-horizon market commentary: daily price movements, analyst up-grades and downgrades, consensus opinion about near-term direction. This information has essentially zero predictive value for individual investors over meaningful time horizons—systematic reviews of financial media consistently show that no source reliably predicts near-term market movements—and its primary effect is to trigger the emotional decision-making (panic selling, euphoric buying) that destroys long-run compounding returns.

The financial Signal that matters is extraordinarily simple and extraordinarily boring: savings rate, cost of investment vehicles, asset allocation relative to time horizon, and tax efficiency. These four variables explain the vast majority of long-run investor outcomes. The rest is noise.

Relational Noise

In relationships, cognitive noise takes the form of second-hand accounts, partial information, and speculative interpretation of behavior. The noise is amplified by the availability heuristic: vivid, emotional, recent information dominates the relationship model, displacing the more statistically reliable signal of behavior patterns observed over years.

The relational Signal test: Does this piece of information—this report from a third party, this interpretation of a single incident, this rumor—actually change the long-run behavioral evidence on which my assessment of this relationship is based? If not, it is noise, and treating it as Signal distorts the relationship model in ways that produce unwarranted conflict and unwarranted trust in equal measure.

7.9 Designing Your Information Environment

The Noise Reduction Protocol provides a periodic audit process. But the more powerful intervention is upstream: the deliberate design of the information environment in which you operate day-to-day, structured so that high-SNR inputs are the default and low-SNR inputs require active effort to reach.

This is the information-environment equivalent of the behavioral economics principle of **choice architecture**: the design of the decision environment so that the default behavior aligns with the desired behavior, without requiring active willpower to sustain. Just as a cafeteria that places fruit at eye level and desserts on a lower shelf increases fruit consumption without removing the choice to select dessert, an information environment designed with deliberate architecture increases high-SNR consumption without requiring constant volitional resistance to noise.

Concrete architectural interventions:

Physical device architecture. Remove social media applications from the home screen of your phone. Not from the phone—the marginal friction of navigating to a buried application folder or a browser is small, but it interrupts the automatic reflex that converts idle moments into noise consumption. The goal is to make the transition from "device in hand" to "noise consumed" require a deliberate step rather than a tap.

Notification architecture. Disable all push notifications except those from the specific individuals whose communications require immediate response. Notifications are the attention-capture mechanism of the information economy; they are designed to interrupt and redirect attention at the platform's discretion rather than yours. Disabling them does not require that you respond to communications more slowly; it requires that you respond on a schedule you control rather than one the platform imposes.

Time-blocking for information consumption. Assign specific windows for consuming news, checking communication channels, and engaging with social media—and confine consumption to those windows. The constraint is not on the volume of consumption but on its timing. Unrestricted access to information at any hour eliminates the natural boundaries that previously modulated consumption; time-blocking restores them. Most people discover that consolidating email to two or three daily windows, rather than maintaining open-access monitoring, produces no meaningful degradation in responsiveness while producing substantial improvement in focused attention.

Threshold filters for new inputs. Before subscribing to any new information source, require it to pass the Signal test in advance: does this source deliver information that directly informs a current priority, develops a skill I have committed to building, or provides verified data about a domain I need to track? If not, declining is a correct architectural decision, not a failure of curiosity. Information sources are easier to add later than to remove once they have established a foothold in your daily attention.

$$Default\ Behavior = Environment\ Design \times Friction$$
$$Profile\ of\ Each\ Choice$$

7.10 The Depth Dial: Adjusting Signal Intensity

The SNR framework addresses which information to consume. The **Depth Dial** addresses how to consume it.

Most information is consumed at what might be called surface depth: skimming, scanning, absorbing the gist without engaging the substance. Surface-depth consumption is efficient for material where the gist is all that matters, but it is destructive when applied to material that generates genuine cognitive value only through deeper engagement. Reading the abstract of a research paper and feeling informed is not the same as reading the full paper and being able to reproduce its argument, evaluate its methodology, and integrate its findings with prior knowledge. The surface provides the illusion of Signal acquisition; the depth provides the actual thing.

The Depth Dial has three settings:

Scan: Appropriate for material being evaluated for relevance. Read enough to determine whether this source warrants deeper engagement. If yes, stop here and schedule deeper consumption at a dedicated time. If no, discard without guilt.

Read: Appropriate for material that has passed the relevance filter and warrants full engagement. Read completely, sequentially, without distraction. Take brief notes on the ideas that change or extend existing understanding. This setting is incompatible with simultaneous phone checking or background audio—the cognitive process of connecting new information to existing knowledge requires focused attention.

Study: Appropriate for material at the core of a current primary goal. Read with deliberate engagement: pause to predict what comes next, summarize sections in your own words without looking, generate questions the material does not answer, connect explicitly to other things you know. The cognitive science of learning consistently demonstrates that effortful engagement of this kind produces dramatically superior retention and integration compared to passive reading at equal time investment. Study mode consumes more time per page but produces more durable knowledge per hour.

The Depth Dial corrects a common information consumption error: applying surface-depth processing to high-value material because high-volume consumption feels more productive than slow, deep engagement with less. It does not feel more productive because it is. It feels more productive because volume is visible and depth is not.

Chapter Logic Check

☐ If I applied the Signal test to every regular information source I currently consume, which three would I immediately cut—and what would I do with the recovered attention?

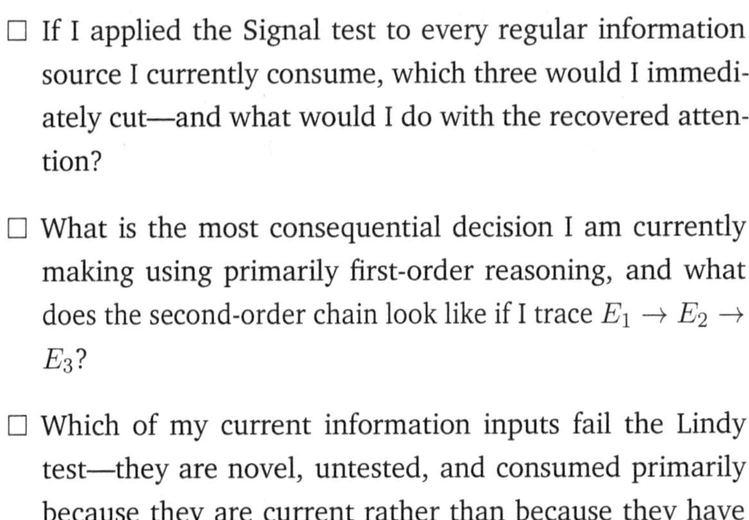

☐ What is the most consequential decision I am currently making using primarily first-order reasoning, and what does the second-order chain look like if I trace $E_1 \rightarrow E_2 \rightarrow E_3$?

☐ Which of my current information inputs fail the Lindy test—they are novel, untested, and consumed primarily because they are current rather than because they have demonstrated durability?

Chapter 8

The Geometry of Connection: Relationship Game Theory

"Hell is other people."
—Jean-Paul Sartre, *No Exit*

"Heaven is also other people."
—almost everyone, eventually

8.1 The Longest-Running Experiment in Human Happiness

In 1938, Harvard University launched what would become one of the longest-running longitudinal studies in the history of social science. The Harvard Study of Adult Development began tracking the lives of 268 Harvard sophomores and, later, a parallel group of inner-city Boston residents. Researchers collected health data, recorded interviews, administered psychological assessments, and followed the subjects for decades—eventually tracking their children and grandchildren as well, producing a dataset that spans more than eighty years of human lives.

The study's central finding, reported by its directors in multiple publications and summarized by Robert Waldinger in a widely watched TED talk, is both simple and frequently discounted by people who have not yet spent eighty years discovering it for themselves: **the quality of your relationships is the single most powerful predictor of your health, happiness, and longevity.** Not wealth. Not fame. Not professional achievement. Not even genetics, though genetics matter considerably. The strength of the social bonds a person maintains through middle age predicts their physical health, cognitive function, and subjective wellbeing in old age with more reliability than almost any other variable the researchers measured.

The study also found something that complicates the usual frameworks for relationship advice: it is not the number of relationships that matters, or even their apparent depth. It is their **quality as experienced**—the degree to which they feel reliable, authentic, and safe. A person with three genuinely close relationships fares better than a person with fifteen superficial ones. A marriage experienced as a source of genuine security produces better health outcomes than a marriage experienced as a source of chronic low-grade conflict, even when both marriages are intact by conventional measures.

This finding positions relationships not as a pleasant supplement to the practical work of life but as a **foundational infrastructure**—a stock, in the systems language of Chapter Three, upon which everything else compounds. The mathematical thinker who has understood compounding, expected value, and constraint optimization but has not understood the dynamics of relationships has optimized the instrument and neglected the foundation on which the entire structure rests.

This chapter provides the frameworks. Not because relationships can be reduced to formulas—they cannot—but because the patterns that distinguish stable, high-quality relationships from deteriorating ones are systematic enough to be modeled, and models provide leverage that intuition alone does not.

8.2 The Ratio That Predicts Everything

John Gottman, a psychologist at the University of Washington, spent more than four decades conducting some of the most methodologically rigorous research on relationships in the history of the social sciences. His laboratory—nicknamed the "Love Lab" by the press—used a combination of behavioral observation, physiological measurement, and longitudinal follow-up to study couples in fine-grained detail.

Gottman's finding that attracted the most public attention was his claimed ability to predict, with high accuracy, which couples would divorce—based on observing a single fifteen-minute conversation. The prediction was not based on the content of the conversation, or on the presence or absence of conflict. It was based on a **ratio**.

$$Stability\ Ratio = \frac{Positive\ Interactions}{Negative\ Interactions} \geq 5$$

In couples who remained happy and together, positive interactions—moments of genuine warmth, humor, affection, interest, validation, and playfulness—outnumbered negative interactions by at least $5:1$. In couples who divorced or remained unhappily together, the ratio fell below this threshold, often approaching $1:1$ or lower.

The ratio is important for several reasons beyond its predictive power.

First, it is **structural rather than personal**. A ratio of 3 : 1 is not evidence that two people are wrong for each other. It is evidence that the positive flow rate into the relationship stock is insufficient relative to the negative flow rate. This is a systems diagnosis, not a character diagnosis, and it points toward a structural intervention: increase the positive flow rate. Not by eliminating conflict—conflict is a normal and sometimes necessary feature of close relationships—but by ensuring that the positive context surrounding the conflict is substantial enough to absorb it without destabilizing the overall account.

Second, the ratio reveals the **asymmetric weight of negative interactions**. In financial accounting, a loss of $100 reduces the account by exactly $100, and a gain of $100 restores it. In relationship accounting, the mathematics are less symmetric. Research on negativity bias suggests that negative emotional events are weighted approximately three times as heavily as equivalent positive ones—meaning a single harsh criticism may require three or more expressions of warmth to restore the emotional account to its pre-criticism level. This asymmetry is why the 5 : 1 ratio is necessary for stability: the mathematical reality of negativity bias means that a 1 : 1 ratio is actually a net negative, and stability requires consistently positive excess.

Third, the ratio operates at the level of **micro-interactions**: not dramatic gestures, but small daily moments of acknowledgment, interest, and genuine connection. These constitute most of a relationship's actual texture. The research consistently shows that grand romantic gestures do not compensate for a chronic deficit of small positive interactions. The question is not whether you occasionally do something significant. It is what the ratio looks like on an ordinary Tuesday.

8.3 The Prisoner's Dilemma and the Iterated Game

Game theory models strategic interactions as **games**—formal structures in which players choose strategies, strategies interact to produce outcomes, and outcomes are assigned payoffs. The most famous example, the **Prisoner's Dilemma**, captures a fundamental tension that appears across an enormous range of real-world interactions.

The setup: two players each face a binary choice—cooperate or defect. If both cooperate, each receives a moderate reward. If both defect, each receives a moderate punishment. If one cooperates and one defects, the defector receives the maximum reward and the cooperator receives the maximum punishment.

The Nash equilibrium of the single-play Prisoner's Dilemma—the combination of strategies from which neither player would unilaterally deviate—is mutual defection. Even if each player knows that mutual cooperation would produce a better collective outcome, the individual incentive to defect is dominant: regardless of what the other player does, defecting produces a higher payoff for the individual. The logic is airtight. The outcome is collectively suboptimal.

The resolution comes when the game is **iterated**—played repeatedly between the same two players, with each player able to observe and respond to the other's previous choices.

In Robert Axelrod's landmark computer tournaments of the 1980s, programs embodying different strategies competed in iterated Prisoner's Dilemmas. The winning strategy, in both initial tournaments and subsequent replications, was strikingly simple: **Tit-for-Tat**, submitted by Anatol Rapoport. Tit-for-Tat cooperates on the first move, then does whatever the other player did on the previous move. It cooperates when the other cooperates. It defects when the other defects. It forgives immediately when the other returns to cooperation.

The strategy's success was analyzed extensively and found to depend on four properties:

1. **Nice:** It never defects first—it does not exploit.

2. **Retaliatory:** It responds to defection with defection—it cannot be exploited.

3. **Forgiving:** It returns to cooperation as soon as the other player does—it does not hold grudges.

4. **Clear:** Its behavior is simple enough for the other player to understand and respond to predictably.

> *Long-Run EV = Cooperation + Retaliation When Necessary + Forgiveness + Clarity*

The application to human relationships is not metaphorical; it is structurally exact. Every significant long-term relationship is an iterated game. The players have history, reputation, and the expectation of future interaction. In this context, the single-play incentive to defect is dominated by the iterated incentive to build a cooperative equilibrium, which produces sustained mutual benefit unavailable to defectors.

Tit-for-Tat with an additional property—occasional **unprompted forgiveness**—performs even better in noisy environments where miscommunication can cause unintended defection signals. In practice: when cooperation breaks down due to a misunderstanding rather than genuine malice, breaking the retaliatory cycle with an unprompted cooperative gesture interrupts what would otherwise become a mutually destructive escalation. This is not weakness. It is strategically superior behavior in an iterated game.

8.4 Trust as a Compounding Stock

The systems language of Chapter Three provides the most precise framework available for understanding what relationships actually build over time.

Trust is the central stock of any significant relationship. It accumulates through consistent, reliable, honest interactions and depletes through betrayals, inconsistencies, and the accumulated weight of unrepaired conflicts. Like all stocks, it changes slowly—a trust stock built over years cannot be destroyed in a single incident (though sufficiently severe incidents can cause catastrophic step-function declines), and a depleted trust stock cannot be rebuilt in a single grand gesture (though consistently positive behavior over time can restore it).

The flows into the trust stock include: reliable follow-through on commitments, honest communication even when honesty is costly, demonstrated prioritization of the relationship under conditions of competing demands, and what Gottman calls **turning toward**—the pattern of responding to a partner's bids for emotional connection with attention and engagement rather than turning away or turning against.

The flows out of the trust stock include: inconsistency between stated intentions and actual behavior, selective honesty (sharing information that serves your interests while withholding information that does not), chronic emotional unavailability, and the accumulation of small betrayals—promises unmade, needs unacknowledged, moments of connection declined.

The compounding principle applies directly: small, consistent positive flows into the trust stock produce a compounding base of relationship resilience that can absorb the normal stresses and conflicts of a shared life. Small, consistent negative flows deplete that base in ways that are invisible in any single period and undeniable in aggregate.

$$\text{Trust}(t) = \text{Trust}(t_0) + \int_{t_0}^{t} \left[F_{\text{positive}} - F_{\text{negative}} \right] d\tau \qquad (8.1)$$

The practical implication: the most valuable relational investment is not the dramatic intervention—the grand reconciliation, the lavish gesture—but the consistent maintenance of the flow rate. Show up reliably. Follow through on small commitments. Be honest in low-stakes moments so that honesty in high-stakes moments is not surprising. Respond to bids for connection with attention rather than distraction. These are not romantic prescriptions; they are the flow rates that build the compounding stock.

8.5 The Communication Error and Its Consequences

The majority of relationship conflicts do not arise from genuine differences in values, interests, or care. They arise from failures in the transmission of information between people who, in most cases, wish each other well.

In information theory terms, the relationship channel has a noise coefficient $E_{\text{communication}}$ that degrades the fidelity of transmitted intent:

$$\text{Reception} = \text{Intent} \times (1 - E_{\text{communication}}) \qquad (8.2)$$

When $E_{\text{communication}}$ is high—when the channel is noisy due to mismatched emotional states, different interpretive frameworks, or simple ambiguity of expression—the received message may bear little resemblance to the intended one. A statement of concern is received as criticism. A request for space is received as rejection. An expression of frustration about a situation is received as an expression of frustration about the person.

The mathematical thinker's first question when a message produces an unexpected reaction is not "what did I do wrong?" or "why are they overreacting?" but "what is the current $E_{\text{communication}}$ in this channel, and what is the most probable interpretation of my message given that noise level?"

This reframe has a specific practical consequence: it makes conflict investigation a collaborative problem-solving exercise rather than an adversarial one. The question to the other person is not "why did you react that way?"—which presupposes that the reaction was unreasonable—but "what did you hear?"—which acknowledges the possibility of transmission error and invites joint diagnosis of the noise.

Three practices reduce $E_{\text{communication}}$:

Explicit intent statements: Begin messages that carry significant emotional content by stating the intent before the content. "I want to tell you something that might be hard to hear, and I'm saying it because I care about the relationship, not because I want to hurt you." The intent statement calibrates the receiver's interpretive frame before the message arrives, reducing the probability of misinterpretation.

Reflection before response: Particularly in high-stakes exchanges, pause to reflect back what you heard before responding to it. Not mimicking—genuine paraphrase of the interpreted meaning. If the paraphrase is accurate, the conversation can continue. If it is not, the speaker can correct the transmission error before the dialogue has proceeded in a wrong direction.

Repair attempts: Gottman's research identifies **repair attempts**—any action or statement designed to de-escalate a conflict or restore emotional connection during a difficult interaction—as one of the strongest predictors of relationship health. Effective relationships are not conflict-free; they are conflict-responsive. The capacity to de-escalate, to introduce humor or acknowledgment at a moment of tension, to reach across the emotional distance with a gesture of connection, is the single most valuable communication skill in a long-term relationship.

8.6 Social Network Structure and Its Consequences

Beyond the bilateral relationship, the structure of a person's social network—the pattern of who is connected to whom—has predictable consequences for their access to information, opportunities, and support.

Mark Granovetter's foundational 1973 paper, "The Strength of Weak Ties," established a counterintuitive finding:

weak ties—acquaintances, distant connections, people known through intermediaries rather than directly—are often more valuable sources of new information and opportunity than strong ties. Strong ties tend to be clustered: your close friends know most of the same people you do and are exposed to most of the same information. Weak ties bridge different social clusters and therefore carry information that your strong-tie network does not already possess.

The practical implication for career development and opportunity is significant: the most valuable new opportunities—job openings, introductions, ideas—disproportionately arrive through weak ties rather than strong ones. A strong-tie network provides depth and emotional support; a diverse weak-tie network provides breadth and novel information. Both are necessary; they are not substitutes.

This has a specific prescription for social investment: deliberately maintain a diverse range of weak-tie connections across different industries, disciplines, and social contexts. Not superficially—with the hollow LinkedIn connections that carry no actual relationship substance—but genuinely, through periodic low-cost interactions that keep the connection alive without requiring the high maintenance of a strong tie. The occasional message, the shared article, the genuine expression of interest in the other person's work. This is relational investing: allocating modest but consistent attention to the weak-tie portfolio that generates the highest variance of novel opportunity.

8.7 Relationships Across Three Domains

Romantic Partnerships

The Gottman research, the trust-stock framework, and the iterated game analysis converge on a small number of highly actionable prescriptions for romantic partnerships. Maintain the 5 : 1 ratio by increasing positive micro-interactions rather than trying to eliminate conflict. Treat repair attempts seriously—a partner's bid to de-escalate a difficult moment is not weakness but skill, and responding to it with continued escalation depletes the repair capacity of the relationship. Apply Tit-for-Tat with forgiveness: respond to genuine hurtful behavior with clear acknowledgment of its impact, but return to cooperation when the other person demonstrates genuine change, without carrying the weight of past defection forward indefinitely.

Professional Relationships

In professional contexts, the trust-stock framework applies with equal precision and somewhat higher stakes, because professional trust is both more difficult to rebuild and more visible in its absence. The primary positive flows in professional trust building are: reliability (doing what you said you would do, by when you said you would do it), competence in your domain, and genuine investment in the other person's success rather than merely in the transaction at hand. The primary trust depletors are: inconsistency between stated priorities and actual behavior, credit allocation errors, and the small failures of follow-through that accumulate below the threshold of explicit complaint.

Friendship and Community

In friendships and community relationships, the most common source of deterioration is not conflict but **neglect**—the slow decline in flow rate that produces a depletion of the trust and connection stock without any single moment of rupture. Friendships that are not actively maintained tend to decrease in connection quality even without negative events, because the positive flow rate has dropped below the natural outflow produced by geographic distance, schedule divergence, and the competing demands of career and family.

The corrective is the same as in any stock-flow system: identify the flow rate required to maintain the stock at the desired level, and design a system—a recurring calendar reminder, a standing habit of periodic outreach—that sustains that rate without requiring daily motivation to generate it. The friendship maintained by a system is maintained more reliably than the friendship maintained by intention alone, for the same reason that financial savings automated by direct deposit are accumulated more reliably than savings requiring monthly volitional decisions.

8.8 The Forgiveness Calculus

One of the most mathematically important and emotionally difficult aspects of iterated relationships is the management of repair after conflict. Gottman's research identifies the capacity for repair as the single strongest predictor of long-term relationship health—more predictive than the frequency of conflict, more predictive than communication style, more predictive than compatibility of values.

Repair is not the same as forgiveness in the philosophical sense. It is the specific behavioral sequence that restores the relationship to a cooperative equilibrium after a defection event—a conflict, a betrayal, a moment of withdrawal or harshness. The mathematics of repair are governed by the trust stock framework: the event depleted the stock; repair is the process of restoring the outflow damage through deliberate positive flows.

Three features of effective repair have clear systemic grounding.

Timeliness. The longer the interval between the conflict and the repair attempt, the more the trust stock continues to deplete through rumination, narrative construction, and the absence of positive flow. A repair that begins within hours is addressing a smaller deficit than one that begins after weeks of silence and accumulated resentment. The mathematics favor immediacy.

Proportionality. The repair must be calibrated to the severity of the depletion event. A minor friction requires a minor repair; a significant breach requires a proportionally significant investment. The common error is under-repair—making a gesture that would be appropriate for a smaller event but insufficient for the actual damage done. Under-repair signals either a failure to accurately assess the impact or an unwillingness to invest the required effort, both of which generate secondary trust depletion.

Specificity. Generic apologies ("I'm sorry for everything") produce less trust restoration than specific acknowledgment of what was done, why it was harmful from the other person's perspective, and what behavior will change. Specificity signals that the analysis has been done—that the event has been processed with sufficient attention to generate a meaningful account of what went wrong and a credible basis for expecting different behavior. Vague repair is structurally similar to vague goals: it provides the sensation of resolution without the substance.

$$\Delta T_{\text{repair}} = (\text{Acknowledgment Specificity}) \times (\text{Behavioral Change Credibility}) \times \text{Timeliness} \tag{8.3}$$

The forgiveness calculus does not prescribe that every repair will succeed—some depletion events cause damage that no repair can fully reverse. But it does prescribe the conditions that maximize repair effectiveness, and it reframes forgiveness not as a moral requirement but as a systems-maintenance decision: restoring the trust stock benefits both parties, because both parties' long-run expected value in the relationship depends on the trust stock level.

8.9 Relational Investment Strategy

The systems framework yields a precise and actionable approach to what might be called **relational investment strategy**: the deliberate allocation of social time and attention across relationships, optimized not by intensity of feeling but by the structure of the stocks being maintained and built.

Most people's relationship investment follows an implicit strategy of **salience**: relationships receive attention when they demand it, primarily through crises, requests, or the calendar accidents that produce encounters. This strategy guarantees under-investment in relationships that are stable (because stable relationships do not demand attention), under-investment in weak ties (because weak ties do not demand attention), and over-investment in relationships that are chronically turbulent (because turbulent relationships demand constant attention regardless of their long-run value).

A deliberate relational investment strategy begins by mapping the relationship portfolio across three tiers.

Tier 1: Core relationships are the small number (typically three to eight) of relationships in which the trust stock is highest, the positive flow rate is highest, and the expected long-run value is greatest. These relationships warrant the highest regular time investment and are the most important to protect from neglect. The error most commonly made with Tier 1 relationships is treating their strength as permission to reduce the flow rate—assuming that a strong trust stock will sustain itself without continued investment. Strong trust stocks deplete under neglect exactly as weaker ones do; the process is just slower and less visible.

Tier 2: Active development relationships are relationships with significant potential value—whether emotional, intellectual, or professional—that are not yet at Tier 1 depth. Building a Tier 2 relationship into Tier 1 requires sustained positive flow investment over a period typically measured in years. The allocation question is how much of the discretionary social attention to invest in building new Tier 2 relationships versus maintaining existing Tier 1 ones.

Tier 3: The weak-tie portfolio is the diverse network of acquaintances and distant connections described in the Granovetter framework. These require minimal but consistent investment: periodic low-cost interactions that maintain the connection without consuming significant time. The value of the weak-tie portfolio is not in any individual relationship but in the aggregate breadth of the network—the diversity of information and opportunity it provides access to.

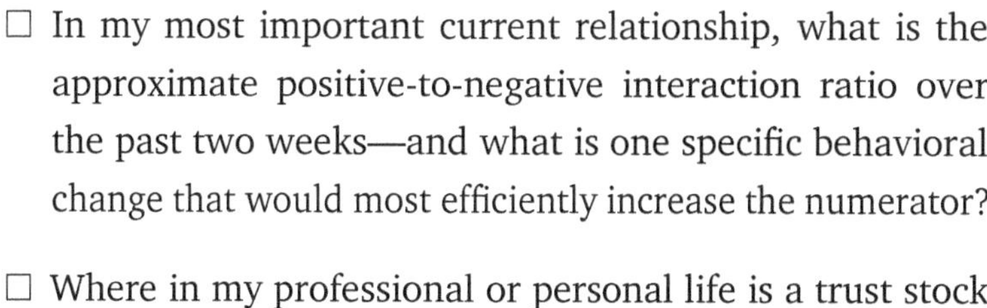

Relational Wealth = (Tier 1 Depth) + (Tier 2 Pipeline) + (Tier 3 Breadth)

The relational investment strategy is periodically reviewed, exactly as a financial portfolio is. Life changes—geography shifts, shared contexts dissolve, priorities evolve—alter the optimal allocation. Relationships that were once Tier 1 may require conscious effort to maintain at that level across significant life transitions; others that were Tier 2 may naturally deepen into Tier 1 through shared experience. The strategy is not a permanent classification but a current best answer to the question: given my finite social attention, what allocation produces the greatest compounding of relational wealth over the next three to five years?

Chapter Logic Check

☐ In my most important current relationship, what is the approximate positive-to-negative interaction ratio over the past two weeks—and what is one specific behavioral change that would most efficiently increase the numerator?

☐ Where in my professional or personal life is a trust stock being depleted by a pattern of small negative flows that I have not yet addressed, because no single incident has been severe enough to demand attention?

☐ Which of my weak-tie connections—the acquaintances and bridge relationships that connect me to different social clusters—have I not contacted in more than six months, and which one would be most valuable to reactivate with a genuine, low-cost interaction this week?

Chapter 9

Career Vectors: Finding Your Direction

"Strategy is about making choices, trade-offs; it's about deliberately choosing to be different."
—Michael Porter

9.1 The Busy Person Going Nowhere

There is a particular kind of professional exhaustion that has nothing to do with insufficient effort. The person experiencing it is not lazy. They are, by most observable measures, exceptionally hard-working—consistently among the first to arrive, the last to leave, the most reliably responsive to messages, the most willing to take on additional work. And yet, despite this sustained, genuine effort, their career trajectory is flat. Promotions come slowly or not at all. The work that would matter most never quite gets done. Five years of intensive effort has produced five years of experience but not the compounding progression they expected.

The diagnosis, in most such cases, is not insufficient magnitude. It is misaligned direction.

In physics, a **vector** is a mathematical quantity defined by two properties: magnitude (its size or intensity) and direction (its orientation in space). A vector with enormous magnitude but no direction is just a scalar—a number without spatial meaning. A force applied at the wrong angle produces displacement primarily in the wrong direction. And in the language of vector multiplication, the component of effort that contributes to forward progress is:

$$d_{\text{effective}} = |\vec{F}| \cos \theta \qquad (9.1)$$

Where θ is the angle between the direction of the force and the direction of the desired displacement.

When $\theta = 0°$, all effort contributes to forward progress. When $\theta = 90°$, effort is perpendicular to the goal and produces zero progress regardless of its magnitude. When $\theta > 90°$, effort actively works against the desired direction.

The person working intensively on tasks that are not on the critical path of their professional advancement is experiencing θ close to $90°$. They are generating significant force, expending significant energy, and producing near-zero effective displacement. The solution is not more effort. It is a rotation of the vector.

9.2 The Physics of Hustle

$$\boxed{\textit{Effective Progress} = |\vec{Effort}| \times \cos(\theta)}$$

The career vector framework demands two distinct analyses, typically performed separately but most usefully performed together.

Magnitude analysis asks: How much total effort am I investing? Is the rate of effort sustainable? What is the quality of effort—is it deep, focused, skills-building work, or is it reactive, shallow, primarily output-generating without developing the underlying capabilities?

Direction analysis asks: What does the market currently value? Where is the actual demand for the capability I am developing? What are the criteria by which advancement decisions in my field are made, and how closely does my current work align with those criteria?

The second analysis is harder and less comfortable than the first, for a specific reason: direction analysis requires engaging honestly with external reality rather than internal conviction. Many people work intensively in directions they find personally meaningful, intrinsically interesting, or socially proximate—without adequately testing whether those directions are valued in the domains where advancement is determined.

This is not an argument for cynical opportunism—for abandoning meaningful work in favor of purely market-driven calculation. It is an argument for **informed direction**: the habit of periodically measuring the angle between your effort and the market's current demand, and asking honestly whether that angle is serving your goals. If it is, proceed with full confidence. If it is not, the question is whether the angle can be rotated—not by abandoning what you value but by finding the orientation of your skills that intersects with where value is currently concentrated.

9.3 The Market Demand Map

Direction analysis requires understanding what the market actually values, which is not the same as what the market says it values. Job postings describe the candidate; the actual hiring decision often reveals different criteria. Performance review criteria describe what the organization claims to reward; the actual promotion decisions reveal what it actually rewards.

The most reliable method for building an accurate market demand map is the **outcome audit**: for the people who have achieved the outcomes you want to achieve, what did they actually do, specifically, in the five years before achieving them? Not what they say they did in retrospect—retrospective accounts are subject to the same narrative construction bias that makes autobiographies unreliable guides. What is verifiable in the record: what projects, what skills demonstrated, what relationships built, what outputs produced?

The outcome audit is uncomfortable because it often reveals that the activities most consistently associated with the desired outcome are not the ones you are currently prioritizing. This is useful information. The gap between what the audit reveals and what you are currently doing is the θ angle made visible.

The audit also reveals the **critical path**: the sequence of capabilities, relationships, and outputs that most directly connects current position to desired outcome, in the most efficient order. The critical path is the direction in which the vector should be oriented.

9.4 Skill Stacking: Manufacturing Rarity Through Intersection

In most professional domains, the competition for the top tier of any single skill is intense, prolonged, and uncertain. The probability of landing in the top 1% of performers in a mature, well-defined field—law, surgery, professional athletics—is low for most practitioners, not because they lack effort or talent, but because the competition for those positions draws from a large, highly motivated pool of able people.

There is a mathematical alternative to this competition that most professionals never consider: **skill stacking**—the deliberate combination of two or more complementary skills that creates a rare and valuable intersection.

If the probability of reaching the top 10% in Skill A is $P(A) = 0.10$, and the probability of reaching the top 10% in the complementary Skill B is $P(B) = 0.10$, and the two skills are approximately independent, then the probability that any given person combines top-10% performance in both is:

$$P(A \cap B) = P(A) \times P(B) = 0.10 \times 0.10 = 0.01 \qquad (9.2)$$

One percent. The intersection of two top-10% skills produces a combination that occurs in approximately one person in a hundred—without requiring top-1% performance in either skill individually.

Add a third complementary skill—$P(C) = 0.10$—and the combined rarity is:

$$P(A \cap B \cap C) = 0.10^3 = 0.001 \qquad (9.3)$$

One person in a thousand. Not because of exceptional performance in any single domain, but because of the rarity of the specific *intersection*.

The strategic implication: if you are already in the top 10% of your primary domain, the highest-leverage investment may not be the effort required to move from the 10% to the 5%—a marginal improvement in an already strong position. It may instead be developing a complementary skill that creates a rare intersection, moving you from a competitive position in a crowded field to a nearly unique position in a small, high-value niche.

$$\textit{Professional Rarity} = P(\textit{Skill}_1) \times P(\textit{Skill}_2) \times P(\textit{Skill}_3)$$

The skill stacking strategy works best when the skills are **complementary rather than redundant**—each amplifies the value of the others rather than merely adding parallel capabilities. The most powerful combinations bridge domains that rarely communicate with each other: the engineer who develops genuine communication skill; the artist who develops quantitative reasoning; the domain expert who develops the ability to teach and translate. Each bridge carries knowledge and methods across a gap that most practitioners never cross, creating value that neither side can supply alone.

9.5 The Human Capital Investment Decision

Professional development decisions—which skills to build, which credentials to pursue, which roles to take for developmental rather than immediate financial reasons—are investment decisions. They can be analyzed with the same Expected Value framework from Chapter Five.

The compound growth formula from Chapter Six applies directly: professional skill is a stock that grows through deliberate practice, compounds through application, and generates returns that themselves fund further development. The time to begin developing a high-leverage skill is not when the return on that skill is already visible in the market. It is as early as possible—because the earlier the investment, the longer the compounding runway.

Consider two people deciding whether to invest 500 hours in developing a complementary skill. The investment has an uncertain payoff—perhaps a 60% probability of producing a meaningful career shift within three years and a 40% probability of producing modest benefit only. The EV calculation:

$$EV = 0.60 \times V_{\text{career shift}} - 0.40 \times C_{\text{time invested}} \qquad (9.4)$$

If the career shift is valued at five years of compounding earnings uplift and the time cost is the opportunity cost of 500 hours, the EV is almost certainly positive for a mid-career professional—even at the 60% probability estimate. The more important variable is often not the probability but the **asymmetry:** if the downside is bounded (500 hours, modest return) and the upside is unbounded (career trajectory shift that compounds for decades), the option value of the investment is high regardless of the exact probability.

9.6 Asymmetric Bets: The Non-Linear Career Move

In conventional career thinking, the dominant mode is risk minimization: take predictable steps, accumulate incremental gains, avoid the costly failures that can set a career back. This is a reasonable first approximation for managing downside, but it systematically undervalues a class of opportunities with profoundly different return structures.

An **asymmetric bet** is an action in which the potential upside is substantially larger than the potential downside—in mathematical terms, an action where $V_{\text{win}} \gg C_{\text{loss}}$, even if $P_{\text{win}} < 0.5$.

In career contexts, asymmetric bets share a characteristic structure: the cost is bounded and recoverable (a defined investment of time, the willingness to tolerate temporary uncertainty or discomfort), while the benefit, if it materializes, produces a durable shift in trajectory that compounds forward indefinitely.

Examples of high-asymmetry career moves:

- **Writing and publishing** in your domain. The cost is hours invested. The potential upside is a durable public demonstration of expertise and inbound opportunities that could not have been predicted in advance.

- **Building something original**: a tool, a product, a methodology, a body of research. The cost is the time and discomfort of creation. The potential upside is intellectual property, reputation, and the compounding returns of ownership rather than pure employment.

- **Cultivating a relationship** with a person whose work you genuinely admire and whose domain is adjacent to yours. The cost is the time and social risk of reaching out. The potential upside is a mentorship, collaboration, or introduction that changes the trajectory of your career.

- **Taking a role** that is beneath your current title but on the critical path to a capability you do not yet have. The cost is a temporary status reduction. The potential upside is the skill that makes the next level accessible.

The mathematical argument for allocating a consistent fraction of professional time to asymmetric bets is straightforward: if even one of many low-cost, high-asymmetry investments produces a large positive outcome, the portfolio EV is substantially positive despite most individual bets producing modest returns.

9.7 The Reputation Stock

Professional reputation is a stock, governed by the same dynamics as any other stock in the systems framework. It accumulates through consistent, high-quality output over time; through reliable follow-through on commitments; through the quality of relationships maintained; and through the compound interest of being the person others reliably recommend. It depletes through inconsistency, through public failures of judgment, and through the slow erosion of confidence when the gap between claimed and demonstrated capability becomes visible.

Like all stocks, reputation changes slowly, compounds, and precedes opportunity. In most professional contexts, the opportunity arrives because of the pre-existing reputation stock, not before it. This means that reputation-building investment precedes its return by years, and the patience required to sustain that investment through the Valley of Disappointment is a professional virtue with clear mathematical grounding.

The most reliable positive flows into the reputation stock are: consistent quality of output, generous attribution of credit to others, and the habit of teaching—actively sharing knowledge and capability with others in the field, which builds both the reputation for expertise and the network of people who have directly benefited from it.

9.8 Career Architecture: The Longer View

The career vector framework is most powerful when applied over a multi-year horizon. A career, like any compounding system, produces most of its value in its later phases—after the skills have compounded, the reputation has built, and the network has reached sufficient density to generate opportunities independently of active cultivation.

Early career: Maximize learning rate (r in the compound formula) even at the cost of near-term compensation. The principal being invested is skill and adaptability. The highest-leverage early career decisions maximize the rate of skill accumulation: exposure to a wide range of problems, rapid feedback cycles, and access to mentors who operate at the level you are aiming for.

Mid career: Identify the intersection that creates your professional rarity and invest deliberately in building the second and third dimensions of the stack. Begin making asymmetric bets consistently. The reputation stock should be growing from the early career investment; direct it toward the niche where the intersection is most valuable.

Later career: The compounding returns on earlier investments arrive. The leverage at this stage is less in skill-building and more in identifying the highest-value applications of accumulated capability—the opportunities where your specific rare intersection is most scarce, and the relationships where genuine collaboration multiplies impact beyond what individual effort produces alone.

9.9 The Network as Career Infrastructure

In Chapter Eight, the Granovetter finding was introduced in the context of friendship: weak ties carry novel information that strong ties do not. In the professional context, this principle has consequences significant enough to constitute a distinct strategic imperative.

The empirical data on job transitions and career advancement consistently confirms Granovetter's original finding: the majority of significant career opportunities—new roles, partnerships, project invitations, funding, introductions to key decision-makers—arrive through weak ties rather than strong ones. The people most likely to connect you to a transformative opportunity are not the people you see weekly; they are the people who move in different circles, have access to different information, and have a specific reason to think of you when a specific opportunity arises.

This has a structural implication for how professional networking is understood and practiced. The conventional model of networking—the deliberate cultivation of visible, powerful people through formal events and transactional relationship-building—is a strategy optimized for the wrong variable. It focuses on building strong ties with high-status individuals, when the evidence suggests that what generates the most career optionality is the breadth of the weak-tie network across diverse domains, not the depth of any single high-status relationship.

The professional network is a system, and like any system, it has stocks and flows. The stock is the accumulated pool of relationships at varying degrees of connection. The flows are the inputs that maintain existing connections and build new ones, and the outputs are the information, opportunities, and referrals that the network generates. A well-maintained, diverse network does not provide value in any given week; it provides compounding option value over years.

$$N_{\text{effective}} = \sum_i P(\text{connection}_i$$

$$\text{generates opportunity}) \times V(\text{opportunity}_i)$$

$$(9.5)$$

Maintaining this system requires what might be called **network hygiene**: the consistent low-cost practice of staying visible and engaged across the network without requiring a specific reason for each interaction. Sharing genuinely useful information with relevant contacts. Expressing genuine interest in others' work when it crosses your attention. Making introductions when two people in your network would benefit from knowing each other. Acknowledging publicly, when appropriate, the contributions of people in your network to your work.

Each of these actions is individually small. Compounded across years and across a network of hundreds of connections, they build a durable infrastructure of professional goodwill

and visibility that generates returns the individual has no way
to predict or schedule.

9.10 Professional Identity and the Direction Question

The career vector framework raises a question that many
professionals find more uncomfortable than any tactical career
question: not "how do I advance?" but "in what direction?"

Direction is the hardest variable in the career equation
because it requires confronting the gap between two things
that are often not the same: what you are good at, and what
you find meaningful. Most people discover this gap not in reflection but in exhaustion—after years of advancing efficiently
in a direction that turned out, on arrival at the destination,
to feel hollow. The problem was not incompetence; it was
a direction chosen on the basis of external signal (what was
available, what was rewarded, what others valued) rather
than on the basis of genuine internal signal (what problems
feel worth solving, what work feels like flow rather than performance).

The mathematical contribution to the direction question
is modest but valuable: the framework for modeling the long-
term consequences of different directional choices. A career
pointed in a direction that aligns with deep intrinsic motivation compounds differently than one pointed in a direction
that does not—not primarily because motivation improves
performance (though it does), but because the intrinsically
motivated person is more likely to sustain the consistency
required for long-run compounding. The zero in the multipli-

cation chain is more likely to arrive from burnout than from bad luck.

This is not a prescription for ignoring market demand and following passion wherever it leads. It is a prescription for identifying the intersection between what you find genuinely meaningful and what the market currently values—the direction in which your vector, pointed at the θ that minimizes the angle to market demand while remaining in the space of meaningful work, produces the greatest forward progress.

The direction question is answered not once but repeatedly, at the review gates described in Chapter Two. Circumstances change, markets change, and personal values mature through experience in ways that cannot be fully anticipated. The directional commitment is a current best answer to a question that benefits from periodic honest reassessment.

9.11 Managing the Transition: Changing Your Vector

A vector can be changed: a different direction applied from the current position forward. But vectors cannot be changed instantaneously in most professional contexts. Direction changes have costs—transition costs, learning costs, the temporary reduction in effective output while the new direction is being established—and they have timelines that are often longer than the urgency of the desire for change implies.

The mathematics of a career transition have three components.

The transition cost is the sum of the investments required to establish credibility and productivity in the new direction: skill development time, credential acquisition, the reduced income or status of a lateral or downward entry into a new domain, and the loss of accumulated domain-specific reputation that does not fully transfer.

The trajectory differential is the expected difference in the compound growth trajectory between the current direction and the new direction, discounted for the probability of successful transition and the time horizon over which the returns are realized.

The break-even point is the time at which the compound returns in the new direction exceed the total transition cost plus the foregone returns in the original direction. Before the break-even point, the transition is a net negative; after it, a net positive.

$$T_{\text{break-even}} : \int_0^T \left[R_{\text{new}}(t) - R_{\text{current}}(t) \right] dt = C_{\text{transition}} \quad (9.6)$$

Most people either overestimate the break-even time (paralysis, staying in a wrong direction too long) or underestimate it (premature transition, insufficient commitment to the transition before abandoning it as unworkable). A realistic estimate of the transition cost—including the full time and capital required to establish genuine productivity in the new direction—is the essential input to making the transition decision correctly.

The other critical variable is timing. Career transitions are more efficient at certain junctures than others: early in a career (when the transition cost is lower because less domain-specific capital has accumulated), at a natural role boundary (when the identity and context change is built into the transition anyway), or when the current direction has hit a confirmed ceiling (when the Limits to Growth archetype from Chapter Three has been definitively reached and no exploitable constraint remains).

Chapter Logic Check

☐ What is the angle θ between my current primary work investment and the direction of greatest market demand in my field—and what specific rotation would reduce that angle?

☐ What is the complementary skill that, added to my strongest current capability, would create the rarest and most valuable intersection I could realistically achieve in the next 18 months?

☐ What is one asymmetric career bet I have been aware of but have not yet made—and what is the honest accounting of why I have not made it?

Chapter 10

The Logic of Investing: Managing Risk and Probability

"The stock market is a device for transferring money from the impatient to the patient."
—Warren Buffett

10.1 Why Most Investors Underperform the Market They Are Invested In

This is one of the most consistent and most counterintuitive findings in empirical finance: the average investor in any given fund earns substantially less than the fund itself returns over the same period. The fund earns 8% per year. The average investor in that fund earns 5% per year, or 4%, or less. How is this possible?

The mechanism is behavioral. Fund investors do not hold their investments passively and collect the fund's returns. They trade: they buy after periods of strong performance (when optimism is high and prices are elevated) and sell after periods of poor performance (when fear is high and prices are depressed). This behavior—the systematic buying high and selling low—is so consistent and so widespread that researchers at Dalbar have tracked it annually for decades and found it persists across market environments, investor types, and investment vehicles.

The mathematical cost is substantial. A $100,000 investment that earns an honest 8% annual return for 30 years grows to approximately $1,006,000. The same $100,000 in the hands of an investor who earns the behavioral average of 5% annual return grows to approximately $432,000. The difference—$574,000—is not attributable to the investments. It is attributable entirely to the decisions made about when to hold and when to sell.

The insight that most self-directed investors most need is not which assets to choose. It is **why they keep making the same behavioral errors**, and how to build systems that prevent those errors from destroying the compounding returns their assets are generating.

This chapter provides that framework. It is not about stock-picking, market timing, or the identification of superior investments. It is about the structural principles—probability, compounding, diversification, position sizing, behavioral architecture—that determine long-run investment outcomes regardless of the specific assets involved.

10.2 The Margin of Safety: Engineering Against Your Own Optimism

Benjamin Graham, whose student Warren Buffett became the most successful investor of the twentieth century, built the intellectual foundation of value investing on a single concept: the **Margin of Safety**.

In structural engineering, a bridge designed to bear 10,000 pounds is built to withstand 30,000. The gap between design requirement and design capacity is the Margin of Safety. It exists not because the engineer expects the bridge to regularly carry three times its design load, but because engineering estimates are uncertain, materials degrade over time, and a bridge that fails under its design load produces catastrophic consequences that a bridge engineered with margin does not.

The investment equivalent:

$$Safety = Value_{Intrinsic} - Price_{Market}$$

When you purchase an asset at its full intrinsic value—paying exactly what the asset is worth based on reasonable estimates of its future cash flows, growth, and risk—your Margin of Safety is zero. A small estimation error, an unexpected adverse development, or a period of reduced market confidence in your asset can push the market price below what you paid, producing a loss that no amount of long-run patience can fully compensate.

When you purchase at a significant discount to estimated intrinsic value—when the market is pricing the asset below what dispassionate analysis suggests it is worth—you have engineered protection against your own estimation errors. Your intrinsic value estimate may be 15% too optimistic and the investment still performs acceptably, because the discount provided a buffer.

The Margin of Safety is not merely a valuation tool. It is an epistemological tool: a formal acknowledgment that your estimates are uncertain, and a structural protection against the consequences of that uncertainty. It converts the question "is this a good investment?" to the more honest question: "is this investment cheap enough relative to its reasonable value range that it remains acceptable even if my analysis is somewhat wrong?"

The stress-test procedure:

1. Estimate intrinsic value under your base-case assumptions.

2. Reduce your revenue or cash flow estimate by 15–20%.

3. Increase your cost or risk estimate by 15–20%.

4. Recalculate intrinsic value under these stressed assumptions.

5. If the stressed intrinsic value still exceeds the market price, the Margin of Safety is genuine. If not, you are betting on your base case being exactly right—and paying for it.

10.3 Modern Portfolio Theory: Why Diversification Is a Free Lunch

Harry Markowitz received the Nobel Prize in Economics in 1990 for a mathematical insight that is simultaneously obvious in retrospect and routinely ignored in practice: **the risk of a portfolio is not the average of the risks of its components.** It is a function of the *correlations* between those components—and by combining assets whose returns are not perfectly correlated, it is possible to reduce portfolio risk without proportionally reducing expected return.

This is the mathematical basis for what Nobel laureate Merton Miller called "the only free lunch in finance": diversification reduces risk without requiring any sacrifice of expected return, provided the diversification is genuine—across assets whose returns respond differently to the same economic conditions.

For two assets with expected returns μ_1 and μ_2, standard deviations σ_1 and σ_2, and correlation coefficient ρ:

$$\mu_p = w_1\mu_1 + w_2\mu_2 \tag{10.1}$$

$$\sigma_p^2 = w_1^2\sigma_1^2 + w_2^2\sigma_2^2 + 2w_1w_2\rho\sigma_1\sigma_2 \tag{10.2}$$

The portfolio expected return μ_p is always the weighted average of the component returns—no free lunch there. But the portfolio variance σ_p^2 contains the correlation term ρ. When $\rho < 1$—when the assets do not move in perfect lockstep—the portfolio variance is less than the weighted average of the component variances. The more negative the correlation, the larger the variance reduction.

The practical implication is direct. Holding ten highly correlated assets—ten technology stocks, for example, all responding to the same macro drivers in the same direction—provides essentially no diversification benefit. In a downturn that affects the technology sector, all ten positions decline together, and the portfolio behaves as if you owned a single concentrated technology position.

Genuine diversification requires assets across categories that respond differently to the same economic conditions: equities and bonds (historically negatively correlated during risk-off environments), domestic and international equities (partially independent business cycles), different sectors (consumer staples and financials respond differently to interest rate changes), and where appropriate, alternative assets that have low correlation with traditional equity and bond markets.

10.4 The Kelly Criterion: How Much to Risk

Knowing that an opportunity has positive expected value is necessary but not sufficient for rational investment. You must also determine **how much** of your capital to allocate to it. This is the position-sizing problem, and it is where many investors with sound analytical judgment nevertheless destroy their long-run returns—by betting too much on good ideas and experiencing the catastrophic drawdowns that result.

The mathematically optimal position size was derived by Claude Shannon's colleague John Kelly at Bell Labs in 1956, originally in the context of maximizing the growth rate of a gambler's bankroll:

$$f^* = \frac{bp - q}{b} = p - \frac{q}{b} \tag{10.3}$$

Where f^* is the optimal fraction of capital to risk, b is the net odds (the profit per unit wagered, so $b = 1$ for an even-money bet that doubles the stake), p is the probability of the favorable outcome, and $q = 1 - p$ is the probability of the adverse outcome.

The Kelly Criterion has two important properties that make it the theoretically optimal position-sizing rule.

Property 1: It maximizes long-run growth rate. Over a long sequence of wagers, no strategy consistently outperforms

Kelly. Strategies that bet more than f^* grow the bankroll faster in the short run but produce catastrophic drawdowns that permanently destroy the capital base. Strategies that bet less than f^* grow more slowly without providing proportionally better downside protection.

Property 2: Kelly betting avoids ruin. Because f^* is always a fraction of remaining capital rather than a fixed dollar amount, the Kelly strategy can never go to zero in a sequence of adverse outcomes—each bet is a fraction of whatever remains. This is the mathematical guarantee against ruin that fixed-size betting strategies do not provide.

In practice, investment practitioners frequently use **fractional Kelly**—allocating half or a quarter of the Kelly-optimal fraction—to account for estimation uncertainty in p and b. Because the Kelly formula is highly sensitive to errors in the probability estimate (overestimating p by 10 percentage points can double the recommended position size), and because position sizing errors in the over-Kelly direction are far more dangerous than errors in the under-Kelly direction, conservative application of a fraction of Kelly is widely considered more prudent than full Kelly in real investment contexts.

10.5 Time in the Market vs. Timing the Market

Among the most durable findings in empirical investment research is the cost of missing the market's best days through well-intentioned market timing. A $10,000 investment in the S&P 500 held continuously from January 1, 1995 to December 31, 2024 grew to approximately $200,000. The same investment, but missing only the best 10 trading days in that period, grew to approximately $91,000. Missing the best 20 days produces roughly \$50,000. The best days are not predictable in advance—they cluster around the worst days, in the periods of highest volatility, when the emotional case for being out of the market is strongest.

This finding is not an argument for never selling. It is an argument for the mathematical cost of the behavioral pattern that market timing almost always produces in practice: exiting when fear is high (after a decline, when the best forward returns are often concentrated) and re-entering when confidence is high (after a recovery, when the concentrated returns have already been realized).

$$R_{\text{buy-and-hold}} - R_{\text{market-timer}} = \text{Cost of Missed Best Days}$$

$$(10.4)$$

The investor who stays invested through periods of fear and volatility is not being brave or irrational. They are making the mathematically correct decision based on the evidence that their ability to predict the timing of market recoveries is, like essentially every investor's ability, insufficient to justify the cost of being wrong.

The behavioral architecture that supports staying invested is as important as the intellectual understanding that staying invested is correct. Three structural protections:

Automatic investment. Set up recurring investment contributions that execute regardless of current market conditions or your current emotional state. Automatic investment removes the decision of whether to invest this month from the hands of the emotional system and places it in the hands of a rule established when you were calm.

Do-nothing protocols. Establish explicit rules that prevent trading actions during defined trigger states—specifically, within 48 hours of a significant market decline. The impulse to act in response to a market decline is almost always an impulse to lock in a loss and exit the market precisely when forward returns are most favorable.

Return consumption reduction. The frequency with which you check investment account values is positively correlated with the frequency of trading decisions—and those decisions, on average, reduce returns. Reducing portfolio check frequency from daily to monthly to quarterly reduces the availability of the emotional triggers that generate counterproductive trading behavior.

10.6 Tax Efficiency: The Silent Compounder

Among the variables most undervalued by individual investors, tax efficiency is perhaps the most consequential. The reason is compounding: tax costs paid currently reduce the capital that would otherwise compound forward, and the compounding returns on that foregone capital are permanently lost.

Consider two investors with identical pre-tax returns of 8% annually. Investor A generates primarily long-term capital gains and qualified dividends, taxed at 15–20%. Investor B generates primarily short-term gains through frequent trading, taxed at ordinary income rates of 25–37%. The after-tax return differential may be 2–5 percentage points annually. On a 30-year horizon with compounding, the difference in terminal wealth between these two investors is enormous—not because their investment selections differ, but because of the tax drag on their identical gross returns.

$$A_{\text{after-tax}} = P(1 + r(1 - \tau))^t \qquad\qquad (10.5)$$

Where τ is the effective tax rate on investment returns. The after-tax compound rate $r(1 - \tau)$ is lower than the gross rate r by the factor $(1 - \tau)$, and this difference compounds over time. At $r = 8\%$ and $\tau = 0.30$, the after-tax rate is 5.6%. Over 30 years, a \$100,000 investment at 8% grows to \$1,006,000; at 5.6%, it grows to \$519,000. The 2.4% tax drag costs nearly \$487,000 on a single investment—without any difference in gross investment performance.

The main mechanisms of tax efficiency available to individual investors:

Tax-advantaged accounts (401(k), IRA, Roth IRA, HSA) allow investment returns to compound without annual tax drag. The compound value of a dollar in a tax-advantaged account versus a taxable account is, over a 30-year horizon at typical return and tax rates, often double or more.

Tax-loss harvesting converts unrealized losses in a portfolio into realized losses that offset taxable gains, deferring the tax liability and preserving capital for continued compounding.

Long-term holding converts short-term gains taxed at ordinary income rates into long-term gains taxed at preferential rates, simply through patience.

Asset location places tax-inefficient assets (bonds, REITs, high-dividend stocks) in tax-advantaged accounts and tax-efficient assets (index funds, growth equities) in taxable accounts, reducing the overall portfolio tax drag.

None of these mechanisms requires any superior ability to select investments. They are purely structural—the product of system design, not analytical skill.

10.7 Behavioral Investing: The System That Protects You From Yourself

The most valuable investment management skill is not financial analysis. It is behavioral architecture—the design of investment systems that prevent the documented behavioral errors from destroying the returns that the assets are generating.

A complete behavioral investment architecture has five components.

Written Investment Policy Statement. Before any investment decision is made, document in writing your investment objectives, time horizon, risk capacity, asset allocation targets, rebalancing rules, and the specific conditions under which you will deviate from your standard plan. The act of writing forces precision; the document serves as a reference during periods of emotional intensity when the temptation to deviate is strongest. Reading your own reasoning from a calm moment is a more reliable guide to rational behavior than your reasoning in the moment of fear or euphoria.

Rebalancing Rules. Establish explicit rules for rebalancing the portfolio to target allocations—either on a calendar schedule (quarterly, annually) or when allocations drift beyond defined thresholds (e.g., any asset class deviates more than 5 percentage points from target). Rebalancing mechanically implements the counterintuitive behavior that produces superior long-run returns: selling what has become expensive relative to target and buying what has become cheap. It converts the emotional difficulty of buying after declines into a rule-governed process that executes without requiring emotional courage.

Pre-Committed Holding Periods. For long-term investments, establish minimum holding periods at the time of purchase and record them in the Investment Policy Statement. A pre-committed holding period reduces the availability of the exit option during periods of underperformance, protecting against the behavioral pattern of selling at the worst moment.

Decision Logs. Record every significant investment decision: the date, the asset, the rationale, the probability estimates underlying the decision, and a scheduled review date. When the review date arrives, evaluate the decision on the quality of the reasoning—not just the outcome. This practice builds calibration over time and identifies systematic biases in your investment reasoning before they compound into large losses.

Deliberate Inertia. In investing, unlike most domains, doing nothing is frequently the highest-value action available. Design the investment system so that action requires deliberate effort—a waiting period, a written rationale, a review against the Investment Policy Statement—while inaction is the default. This inverts the typical architecture of brokerage platforms, which are designed to facilitate easy trading, and substitutes an architecture designed to facilitate easy holding.

> *Investment Outcome = Asset Returns × (1 − Behavioral Drag) × (1 − Tax Drag) × Time*

10.8 The Logic of Investing Across Time Horizons

Investment strategy is not one-size-fits-all. The mathematically optimal allocation is a function of time horizon, risk capacity, and the specific goals the capital is intended to serve. Different time horizons imply fundamentally different risk structures.

Short time horizons (capital needed within five years) require capital preservation above return maximization. Variance at the wrong moment—a 30% market decline shortly before you need to withdraw—is not recoverable within the time available. Short-horizon capital belongs primarily in low-variance assets: high-quality bonds, cash equivalents, stable-value funds. The forgone return is the cost of optionality preservation; it is not a mistake.

Medium time horizons (five to fifteen years) allow for a balanced allocation that accepts moderate variance in exchange for moderate expected return. The time is sufficient to recover from most adverse market events, but not sufficient to confidently absorb the full variance of an equity-heavy portfolio without significant risk of a poor sequence of returns near the end of the period.

Long time horizons (fifteen years and beyond) are mathematically unique because the compounding of equity returns over long periods has, historically, reliably dominated the variance risk that short-horizon investors correctly fear. A 30% market decline is painful and newsworthy; over a 30-year time horizon, it is a footnote. The risk to a long-horizon investor is not short-term variance. It is behavioral risk—the probability of making a fear-driven exit during a decline and missing the recovery—and inflation risk, the probability that a capital-preservation allocation fails to grow faster than the erosion of purchasing power.

The age-and-risk heuristic ("hold 100 minus your age in stocks") is a rough approximation of this principle that has the right qualitative direction but wrong quantitative precision for most situations. The correct allocation is not a function of age alone but of time horizon, risk capacity, income stability, and the specific liability structure of the investor's future obligations.

Chapter Logic Check

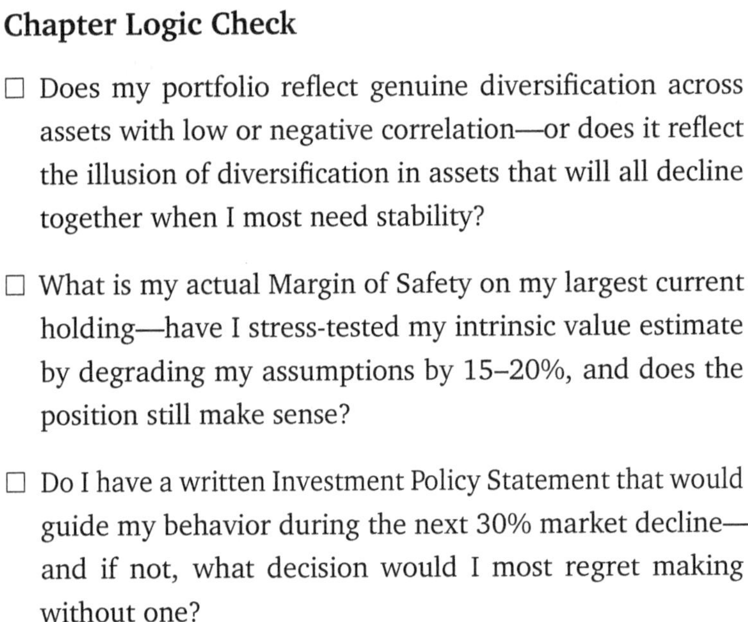

- [ ] Does my portfolio reflect genuine diversification across assets with low or negative correlation—or does it reflect the illusion of diversification in assets that will all decline together when I most need stability?

- [ ] What is my actual Margin of Safety on my largest current holding—have I stress-tested my intrinsic value estimate by degrading my assumptions by 15–20%, and does the position still make sense?

- [ ] Do I have a written Investment Policy Statement that would guide my behavior during the next 30% market decline— and if not, what decision would I most regret making without one?

Chapter 11

The Next Generation: Teaching Logical Agency

"Give a man a fish and you feed him for a day. Teach a man to fish and you feed him for a lifetime."
—attributed to Lao Tzu

11.1 What We Actually Teach When We Teach Children to Think

For most of educational history, the dominant theory of instruction has been **content transfer**: the teacher possesses knowledge; the student lacks it; instruction is the process of moving content from one to the other. Mathematics, in this framework, is a collection of facts and procedures to be transmitted—multiplication tables, formula derivations, equation-solving algorithms. The measure of success is whether the student can reproduce the content on demand.

This model produces students who can pass tests and adults who cannot think. The procedures learned are not generalizable; they apply to the specific problem types for which they were taught, and when life produces problems that do not fit those types, the procedures are useless and the person is helpless.

The alternative framework, which this book has argued for throughout, is **process transfer**: what education should transmit is not primarily the answers but the method of finding them. Not the specific solutions but the reasoning patterns that generate solutions to problems that have never been seen before. Not the formula but the habit of mind that asks: what are the variables? What are the constraints? What does the structure of this problem imply about the structure of its solution?

The most important thing you can do for any young person in your life—child, student, mentee, or younger colleague—is to model and teach this habit of mind explicitly. Not as a special program or a supplementary curriculum, but as the default way you respond to the problems that arise in daily life, and the default way you invite them to respond as well.

11.2 Teaching the Variable Audit to Children

The Variable Audit from Chapter One is not a complex tool. Its complexity is in the precision it demands, not in the cognitive difficulty of the process. Children as young as seven or eight can perform a meaningful version of it, provided the scaffolding is appropriate.

The pediatric version of the Variable Audit proceeds through four questions, asked in conversation rather than written on a worksheet:

"What exactly do you want?" This question, asked with genuine patience and interest rather than impatience, teaches children that vague desires ("I want to be happy," "I want things to be better") are the first obstacle to getting what they want. The process of answering it precisely—"I want to save $40 to buy this specific item by this specific date"—is the first application of precision thinking to a real personal objective.

"What do you need to make it happen?" This surfaces the variables in a form accessible to a child's vocabulary. It distinguishes what the child can influence from what they cannot, and it begins the process of directing attention toward the levers.

"What might get in the way?" This names the constraints and the risks—gently introducing probabilistic thinking through the back door of anticipation. The child who has already thought through what might go wrong is less likely to be derailed when it does.

"What's the first thing you can actually do?" This is the bridge from analysis to action, and it teaches that analytical thinking is not separate from practical agency—it is the preparation for it. The first action should be specific, immediate, and within the child's current capacity.

$$Outcome = \frac{Input \times Skill}{Constraint}$$

The mathematical vocabulary does not need to be introduced at first. The habit of mind is what matters. Once the habit is established through repeated application to the natural problems of childhood—the toy that costs too much, the friendship that is complicated, the school project that feels impossible—the mathematical formalization of that habit becomes a natural and welcomed clarification rather than an alien imposition.

11.3 Debugging the Process: Reframing Failure as Information

In conventional schooling, a wrong answer is a red mark—a judgment of the person. In conventional parenting, a child's failure is frequently experienced as a reflection of the parent, triggering responses that communicate shame, inadequacy, or disappointment rather than curiosity and problem-solving orientation. Both environments teach children the same lesson: failure is evidence of a defect, to be hidden and minimized rather than examined and corrected.

This lesson is the opposite of what mathematical thinking requires.

In mathematics, an error is not a verdict. It is a **counterexample**: a specific case that demonstrates that the current model is wrong in a specific way, providing information about where the model needs to be revised. The error is not the end of the process; it is a step in the process. The correct response to an error is not shame but investigation: at which point did the reasoning diverge from what the problem required?

Teaching children to debug their failures—to locate the error in the process rather than in their identity—is among the most consequential educational gifts available. The three-category framework:

Input Error: Was the required effort actually supplied? Not as a shaming question but as a diagnostic one. If the answer is no, the correction is straightforward and the child's dignity is intact: the process wasn't completed, not the person.

Process Error: Was the strategy or method flawed, even if the effort was genuine? This category is the most intellectually interesting because it implies that effort and good outcome can be decoupled—that working hard at the wrong approach produces poor results through no character failing. The correction is to find a better approach, which is an intellectually engaging problem rather than a moral one.

Environment Error: Were there genuinely uncontrollable external factors? This category teaches probabilistic realism—the acknowledgment that not all outcomes are within the actor's control, and that a process can be correctly designed and faithfully executed and still produce a bad outcome through variance. This lesson, internalized in childhood, produces adults who can distinguish bad luck from bad judgment and respond appropriately to each.

Separating these three categories converts every failure from a character indictment into a technical problem with a diagnosable cause and a correctable response.

11.4 The Probability of Fear: Teaching Quantitative Courage

Anxiety in children is one of the most consequential cognitive vulnerabilities of modern life. The developmental period in which fear responses are most sensitively calibrated is also the period in which exposure to the most anxiety-generating information environment in history is at its highest—in many households, children are exposed to the full weight of the adult information environment, with none of the epistemic tools to contextualize it.

The mathematical tool that most directly addresses childhood anxiety is **subjective probability**: the habit of assigning an explicit numerical estimate to the likelihood of feared outcomes. It does not require statistical training. It requires only the practice of converting "I am afraid this will happen" into "I estimate there is a __% chance this happens."

The conversation:

"On a scale from 0 to 100, how likely is it that the very worst thing you're imagining actually happens?"

The first time a child attempts this, the number is typically high—50, 70, sometimes 90—because untrained imagination is not calibrated to probability; it is calibrated to vividness. But the process of trying to assign a number forces a comparison: How often has this kind of thing actually happened before? What does the evidence from similar situations suggest? Is the worst case actually the most likely case, or just the most vivid one?

Over time, with gentle practice, children develop an intuition that their feared scenarios typically occupy probability spaces of 3% to 15%—not zero, which would be dishonest, but far from the 60-90% that the emotional experience implies. This calibration does not eliminate fear. It **right-sizes** it: matching the emotional response to the actual probability, rather than to the emotional intensity of the imagined scenario.

The compounding effect of this habit across a childhood is profound. An adult who has spent fifteen years right-sizing their fears through probabilistic reasoning relates to uncertainty differently than one who has spent fifteen years being overwhelmed by it. The anxiety is not gone; it is correctly located, correctly weighted, and workable.

11.5 The Compounding Penny: Making the Invisible Visible

The single most powerful mathematical lesson for a child to encounter is the doubling penny riddle—not because of the financial literacy it conveys, but because of the cognitive model it installs.

Would you prefer $1 million today, or a penny that doubles in value every day for 30 days?

$$V_t = 0.01 \times 2^{t-1} \tag{11.1}$$

On Day 30, the penny is worth $5,368,709.12. The lesson is not that doubling pennies are available. It is that the human intuition about how processes work over time is systematically and dramatically wrong in a specific direction—and that understanding this wrongness is worth more than any specific calculation.

When a child sees the numbers, the intuitive linear model ("the penny will be worth a lot, maybe a thousand dollars") collides with the exponential reality ("more than five million dollars") in a visceral way that neither a lecture about compound interest nor a financial literacy worksheet produces. The collision is the education.

Follow the riddle with explicit identification of the three lessons it contains:

Lesson 1: The Valley of Disappointment is real. After fifteen days, the penny is worth $163.84. If you started the doubling experiment expecting linear progress toward the five-million-dollar destination, fifteen days of penny-scale results would feel like failure. The experiment is not failing. The exponent is loading.

Lesson 2: Consistency is the exponent. If on any single day the doubling does not happen—the penny increases by only 50% instead of doubling—the final value is catastrophically reduced. The power is not in any single day's result but in the unbroken chain. Break the chain once and the exponent resets.

Lesson 3: Back-loading is the nature of compounding. More than half of the total value accumulates in the final three days. This is true of almost every significant life outcome: the majority of the return is concentrated in the later phases, after the early phases have built the base. The person who quits in month fifteen of a twenty-year process has not lost fifteen months of progress. They have lost access to the exponential phase.

11.6 A Mathematical Framework for Raising Autonomous Thinkers

The chapters of this book are not primarily a parenting curriculum. They are a description of the mental habits of effective, adaptive, resilient thinkers—habits that, when modeled consistently in the presence of children, are acquired not through explicit instruction but through the most powerful learning mechanism available to developing minds: observation of a trusted adult thinking well under real conditions.

The parent who responds to a family financial problem by pulling out a notebook and mapping the variables is teaching the Variable Audit without naming it. The parent who responds to a fear by asking "what's the actual probability?" is teaching probabilistic thinking without a statistics lesson. The parent who frames a child's failure as a debugging problem—"let's figure out where the process went wrong"—is teaching the growth mindset in its mathematically precise form.

The explicit tools in this chapter are supplements to this implicit modeling. They formalize and make visible the habits that are being transmitted through the quality of adult thinking in the presence of children. They give children a vocabulary for what they are observing, and that vocabulary provides the scaffold for applying the habits in their own reasoning.

The goal is not to produce children who can solve calculus problems before adolescence. It is to produce adults who approach the unsolved problems of their lives—financial, relational, professional, civic—with the same orientation a mathematician brings to an unsolved equation: not with fear or paralysis, but with the systematic, evidence-responsive, failure-tolerant curiosity of a person who knows how to think.

Chapter Logic Check

□ Am I teaching the people I care for the *answer*, or the *formula* for finding their own answer—and which of those will still be relevant in twenty years?

□ In my own recent experience with failure or difficulty, have I modeled the debugging framework—locating the Input, Process, or Environment error—or have I modeled the shame response I am trying to help others avoid?

□ Which one mathematical concept from this book, if genuinely internalized by a young person in my life, would have the greatest long-run impact on the quality of their decisions—and how could I introduce it through a real situation in the next two weeks?

Appendix: The Mathematical Life Toolkit

The following reference tables consolidate the core frameworks from each chapter. They are designed for repeated use—not as passive reading, but as active worksheets to apply against your current decisions.

A. Core Equations Reference

Chapter	Core Equation
The Precision Mandate	Success = (Target × Time) + Constraints
Calculus of Tradeoffs	$T_{\text{total}} = T_{\text{work}} + T_{\text{rest}} + T_{\text{leisure}}$
Probabilities Over Emotions	$EV = (P_{\text{win}} \times V_{\text{win}}) - (P_{\text{loss}} \times C_{\text{loss}})$
The Law of Compounding	$A = P\left(1 + \frac{r}{n}\right)^{nt}$
Signal-to-Noise Ratio	$SNR = P_{\text{signal}}/P_{\text{noise}}$
Relationship Stability	Stability = Positive/Negative ≥ 5
Career Vectors	$\vec{d} = \text{Magnitude} \times \cos\theta$
Skill Stacking	$P(A \cap B) = P(A) \times P(B)$
Kelly Criterion	$f^* = (bp - q)/b$
Bayesian Updating	$P(A \mid B) = P(B \mid A)\,P(A)/P(B)$

B. The Expected Value Decision Matrix

Use this matrix when facing any significant binary decision. Fill in the four cells, compute EV, and let the mathematics inform—not replace—your judgment.

	You Proceed	You Do Not Proceed
Best Case	Value if it works: $P_{\text{win}} = \underline{\quad}$	Value preserved:
Worst Case	Cost if it fails: $P_{\text{loss}} = \underline{\quad}$	Opportunity cost:
Expected Value	$$EV = (P_{\text{win}} \times V_{\text{win}}) - (P_{\text{loss}} \times C_{\text{loss}})$$ $$= \underline{\quad}$$	

C. The Variable Audit Worksheet

Before engaging with any complex problem, complete the following:

1. **Define the goal.** State it with a number and a deadline.

   ____

2. **Name the variables.** List the factors genuinely within your influence.

   ____

3. **Name the constants.** What genuinely cannot change in your current situation?

   ____

4. **Identify the bottleneck.** Which single constraint is limiting your maximum output?

____

5. **Find the leverage point.** Which variable, if changed, produces the greatest shift in outcome?

____

D. The Bayesian Update Log

Use this log to track belief updates in ongoing high-stakes situations (a partnership, a health protocol, an investment thesis, a career pivot).

Date	Prior Belief	New Evidence	Updated Belief

The goal of this log is not to confirm your initial hypothesis. It is to _track the accuracy of your updating_. Over time, a well-maintained log reveals whether you are genuinely responsive to evidence or merely rationalizing a fixed conclusion.

E. Recommended Reading

The ideas in this book draw on a rich literature. The following works are high-signal, low-entropy resources that have earned their longevity.

- *Thinking, Fast and Slow* — Daniel Kahneman (Probability, Cognitive Bias)

- *The Goal* — Eliyahu M. Goldratt (Theory of Constraints)

- *Against the Gods: The Remarkable Story of Risk* — Peter L. Bernstein (Probability History)

- *The Intelligent Investor* — Benjamin Graham (Margin of Safety, Long-Run Thinking)

- *Fooled by Randomness* — Nassim Nicholas Taleb (Variance, Asymmetry)

- *The Art of Problem Solving, Vols. 1–2* — Richard Rusczyk (Mathematical Reasoning)

- *SuperForecasting* — Philip Tetlock (Bayesian Updating, Calibration)

- *Poor Charlie's Almanack* — Charles T. Munger (Mental Models, Compounding)